MODERN DAY
MENTOR

MODERN DAY MENTOR

The prosperous guide to mentoring, personal growth and leadership

DAMEON K. WROE

Foreword by Billy Wroe, Jr.

Copyright ©2019 by Dameon K. Wroe
Another EP® Publishing Company

All rights reserved. All materials and/or supporting text written in this book are the original work and creation of the author, and are protected by applicable copyright laws on file with the Library of Congress Copyright Office. Any photocopying, reproductions, publications, alterations or duplications of this book and the information contained herein, without the author's or the publisher's expressed written consent, is strictly prohibited by law. It is equally a violation of applicable laws to copy, post, re-post, print or otherwise transfer any text from this book onto any social media website, for any reason whatsoever, without the author's or the publisher's expressed written consent.

To book this author for public speaking engagements, author appearances or book signing events, address all inquiries in writing to:

Another EP® Publishing Company
Post Office Box 300
Walnut, CA 91788-0300
or by email at: anothereppublishingcompany@gmail.com

Cover Design: Michelle Manley
Make-Up Artistry: Erika Sethi
Foreword by: Billy Wroe, Jr.
Photography by: Lyd & Mo

ISBN#: 978-0-9740685-2-7

Printed in the United States
9 8 7 6 5 4 3 2 1

If you purchased this book without a cover, you should know that this book is stolen property. It was reported as "unsold" or "destroyed" to the publisher and neither the author nor the publisher has received any payments for this "stripped book."

Table of Contents

1	A Healthy Diet for Success	1
2	Today's Peer Pressures & How to Cope	13
3	Get Over Yourself!	21
4	How to Identify Your Passions	41
5	So What!	59
6	Time Management & Accountability	75
7	Knock It Off!	87
8	Building Your Financial Future	127
9	Never Give Up!	141
10	Acknowledgments	147
11	In Memory Of	151

Foreword

I am forever honored to have been entrusted with the privilege of writing the foreword for my big brother, Dameon K. Wroe's book, *Modern Day Mentor*. With this being his third book, Dameon takes his gift for writing emotion-evoking poetry, as displayed in both *True Inspirations—A Poetry Collection, Vol. I* and *No Longer Silent—By Way of Poetry*, and seamlessly transitions the power of his words into the arena of self-development! Dameon has experienced a purpose-driven journey throughout his life that has, without a doubt, prepared him to pour out his heart and soul into this innovative and brilliant publication. Dameon has continuously proven that he has a unique ability to overcome extreme adversities…prevailing against all odds.

If there is one area of admiration that I do not express to my brother enough, it is the grit within his mental and intellectual fortitude. I have seen first-hand some of the knock-out blows that life has dealt him, and each time he has gotten back up, dusted himself off and rose to new heights to fiercely meet whatever the challenge may be. Even knowing *this* about him, he will be the first person to tell you that he is not a self-made man. In fact, he would probably go as far as to say that no one is 100% self-made, which is why he regularly gives credit to the community (also known as *his village*) responsible for his ascension to the man he has become today. If you are looking for a mentor, his never-ending will to fight for what he believes in is exactly the mindset that you want rooting for you in your corner. I will let you in on a little secret… that never-ending will to fight for what he believes in—*that* very mindset has been carefully woven into the pages of *Modern Day Mentor*.

In today's world, the mere principles of mentoring are the second greatest teacher, giving way only to one's personal experiences. *Modern Day Mentor* effortlessly steps into the role of a mentor—by teaching us how to appropriately respond to the challenges that we will all inevitably face. Unlike other personal-development books that place the reader in the back seat of the experience, *Modern Day Mentor* builds resonance with the reader by placing them in the driver's seat, as they are given guidance involving true-to-life scenarios, all while using an approach that encourages the reader to choose advice rather than being force-fed a practical solution. In short, it stays true to the "teach a person how to fish for a lifetime" methodology. As a single father, Dameon is now, more than ever, pre-occupied with establishing a solid, intellectual foundation for his own children. As a result, there are many areas of *Modern Day Mentor* that are reminiscent of a conversation that one might have with their *own* father, as an adolescent child attempting to find their way— safely around life's blind spots. As with any healthy mentoring

FOREWORD

relationship, *Modern Day Mentor* establishes a harmonious cadence of patience, urgency, passion and trust that the reader has a well-calibrated compass —capable of pointing them in the direction of the true North of *their* definition of success. You will not only see, but *feel* the compassion in which Dameon approaches reinforcing the levels of confidence necessary to set yourself apart, as you fearlessly face the challenges of the world.

Regardless of what neighborhood you come from, your level of education, your cultural upbringing or where you are in life at this very moment, *Modern Day Mentor* will intentionally empower you to achieve the same measure of success that your efforts deserve. Thank you, big brother, for your integrity and transparency in sharing your story with the world! Continue to be steadfast in your gifted abilities and in your calling to change lives for the better as your leadership journey continues.

Respectfully,
Billy Wroe, Jr.
1stWroe Network—YouTube

CHAPTER 1

A Healthy Diet for Success

Traditional diets have been around for centuries, or as far back as most of us can remember. There are many different variables to consider when exploring the core reasons as to why an individual may feel the need to go on a diet.

In times past, and even in today's society, physical image is a huge factor in the eyes of people from all walks of life. For this reason, many are concerned about how their bodies look and want to ensure that a better looking body makes them feel better about themselves, and makes them feel more socially accepted. Some people may only need or desire to lose a few pounds here and there, while others may need or desire to lose a great deal more weight to avoid adverse health challenges, and quite possibly even death.

Although there are a wide variety of different reasons why a person may need or wish to diet, I will focus on just a few for the sake of making my point. So that you can better understand the tone of this chapter, I will compare the *compulsive* over-eater to the *average* eater who lacks a consistent pattern of healthy eating habits.

Generally speaking, a *compulsive* over-eater is simply awed at the fact that they have such a huge choice of just about any and every kind of food they can get their hands on. In other words, the sky's the limit! Compulsive over-eaters give no extended thought to what they will eat throughout the day and how much of those desired foods that they will consume. The *compulsive* over-eater is not worried about fatty foods, foods high in cholesterol, nor foods that are high in sodium—or which foods lack protein. Whether or not the food tastes good is more of a concern than wondering if they are eating something that is not healthy for them.

On the other hand, the *average* eater may not be as close to facing the same dangers that challenge a compulsive over-eater, but their choices of foods that they *do* consume are not always the healthiest choice. Typically speaking, the average eater may have a more conscious ability to be a little more careful about not eating foods that are clearly unhealthy but, oftentimes, the problem that they face is not taking into consideration the *amounts* of food that they are consuming. Sometimes the things that we deem as being the most complex and comprehensive are actually quite simple to figure out.

It does not take a rocket-scientist to figure out that, if we continue to put things into our bodies that are not good for us then, over a period of time, our bodies will not be functioning at their fullest potential. An expectation of this nature would be pure insanity—performing the same action over and over again, but yet expecting to see a different result. Even though there can never be any solid guarantees of a desired outcome,

CHAPTER 1: A HEALTHY DIET FOR SUCCESS

we stand a much better chance of having a clean bill of health by putting healthier foods into our bodies, and staying mindful of the moderations in which we consume these foods.

Having already sketched a mental picture, with these two comparisons as my focal point, I will now make a practical application to the everyday lifestyle.

Following the advice of a nutritionist or dietitian can absolutely be a design for living a healthier life. Following a healthy diet for success has a similar design, but it serves a more defined and equally rewarding purpose. Just like the unhealthy eater, a person who does not truly have a healthy appetite for success will be easy to identify by how they live their life. Although there are endless examples to consider in all scenarios, hopefully the following examples will help you to identify some of these same types of people that you may encounter from day to day.

The first person that comes to mind is the person who constantly goes around offering their unsolicited advice to other people who have serious problems or issues. This person is quick to tell you how you need to live *your* life, but yet *their* life is tore up from the floor up! This is the same person who is giving *you* advice on how to keep *your* relationship intact, yet they themselves have been divorced multiple times and currently do not have a relationship of their own to maintain. In fact, the reason they cannot mind their own business, is because *your business* is the only life or business that they really have.

The second type of person I'd like to warn you about will never be hard to notice. This is the person in your circle of friends, family, and associates who is forever talking about *themselves* at every possible opportunity. I refer to these kinds of people as having what I call the S.O.S. Syndrome (Stuck On Self).

They will frequently remind you of how much money they make, but never be able to offer you any financial assistance if you should ever fall on hard times. This is the person who has acquired a high or respectable position in the workforce, but can never reach their hand down to pull up another person who is in need of that same 'chance' *they* once needed to take advantage of rewarding career opportunities. This is also the person that you constantly hear bragging about how high up they've gotten in their company yet, when they are asked by a true friend in need to give them a job, all of a sudden there's a hiring freeze within the company.

No matter what industry you're in, you will find that you will always come across co-workers with many of the same characteristics that I've just described. A very essential element pertaining to a healthy diet for success includes knowing what's good for you, and knowing what's not so good for you in the workplace.

Today's workforce is the most diverse and complex it has ever been. From the small, mom and pop business, to the most influential corporations in American history, corporate America is made up of people from all sorts of backgrounds and walks of life. With these things in mind, it is important to realize

CHAPTER 1: A HEALTHY DIET FOR SUCCESS

and understand that you will not always get along with all of your co-workers all of the time, including your supervisors and managers.

Having had a multitude of jobs within corporate America throughout the years, I hope, trust, and pray that the insights I am about to share with you will help you to better understand how to pursue a healthier diet for success for YOU as an individual, no matter what industry or career you may end up with.

I know this may sound a bit harsh in a sense but, **mind your own business!** Too often, we get sucked into situations at work that have nothing to do with us whatsoever. Don't make the mistake of involving yourself in the affairs of other people who do not share the favorable work ethic you have established for yourself. By getting caught up in the wrong crowd of people within your workplace, you can become a target on the radar screen simply because of the people you associate with. I can recall a time when I worked for a fairly big company within the healthcare industry. My assignment at this company was only supposed to last for anywhere between five to six months, although the assignment eventually turned into a regular, full time position that lasted for more than six years.

As my manager was showing me around the department and getting me familiar with the do's and don'ts, she turned to me and said with a smile, "If this is a job you think you might need or want to be at for a long time, the best thing for you to do is try to keep to yourself as much as possible!" At first I didn't understand the importance of what she was telling me but, about a year or two with both my feet in the door, it all made perfectly good sense.

I cannot begin to tell you how many employees I have seen come and go during my employment at, not just the company I mentioned, but with all the companies I've ever worked for. Based on what I had witnessed happening to other employees around me, I made it *my business* to *mind my own business* and not get caught up in the very things that caused those other people to lose their jobs. The attitude I carried around at my job was actually quite simple. When I showed up to work, I made it my business to sit down at my desk and get the work done that my supervisors were counting on *me* to do. Once the rumors and gossiping started flaring up on all sides of me and consuming me, I kept my blinders on and stayed focused on the tasks ahead of me that only I would be held accountable for. Everyone else was out of sight and out of mind.

When I clocked in for work and was ready to start my day, I made certain that, no matter what adversities the day was about to present to me, I did not have *my* name caught up in a bunch of office drama that would have compromised my integrity and the work ethic that I wanted so desperately for my supervisors to notice. You see, from day one of being at this company, I had a goal and a game-plan.

The game-plan was to show my supervisors and managers that, once they had given me a task, I was off and running with it and did not have to be told repeatedly or reminded on numerous occasions to get it done. I was a worker who had developed a reputation for doing *quality* work, and putting

CHAPTER 1: A HEALTHY DIET FOR SUCCESS

my best foot forward at all times. I was determined to let my work speak for itself, and that's exactly how I survived at this company for as long as I did.

Whatever great things you set out to accomplish for yourself, always consider the advice of anyone who admonishes you to have a *goal*, a *proper mindset* <u>AND</u> a *game-plan* in place. In essence—the *goal* is the actual target that you are trying to hit on your road to success…the *mindset* **and** the *game-plan* are key factors in the actual process that you will have to follow in order to reach that goal.

As was suggested to me, I pretty much kept to myself as much as humanly possible. On most jobs that I've had over long periods of time, I made it my business to stand out as a *leader* and not as a follower. When "the in-crowd" was gathered together in the break room - joking together, laughing and giggling together, sharing stories about what each one did over the weekend, and so on, I was taking my lunch out to my car and enjoying it in *literal* peace and quiet. As far as staying off the radar of unnecessary drama, my theory has always been, "Out of sight…out of mind!"

In the workplace, no matter what industry, there will always be a time where someone throws you under the bus, just to keep themselves out of potentially hot water with the boss. But when people that you work with know that you have a reputation for keeping to yourself and being a quiet person, it makes it more difficult for others to believe that you would have even said or done the negative things that some people may eventually accuse you of saying or doing.

Here are a few tips to remember that can help you to better understand the type of attitude and/or demeanor that will prove to be an asset to you on your road to success.

Always strive to be a leader and not a follower. If everyone else in your office appears to be running 'south,' then don't be afraid to step out on faith and run 'north.' If there are a group of employees in your office that are oftentimes being loud, unruly, or disturbing the atmosphere of others around them who are working, do not join in the chaos with them. Stay far away from people who clearly demonstrate, by their actions, that they are negative and inconsiderate.

These people will not be hard to find. They are the people who oftentimes never have a smile on their face or a good word to say to or about you. They are the people you've seen in and around your office for years, and have never felt the need to say so much as, "Good morning."

During my years spent in network marketing, I have heard this expression on many occasions, "If you buy someone else's opinion, you will eventually buy their lifestyle!" The more I thought about this statement, I found it to be painfully true.

If your goal in life is to be a millionaire someday, then you should seek the advice or guidance of someone who has already made a million dollars. If your goal is to become a successful doctor or nurse, then you should not seek the advice or wisdom of a person who only has the experience of being a plumber or a janitor.

If ever you feel the need or the urge to stand out at your present place of employment, let your superiors see that you are indeed different. Let them see that you have what it takes

CHAPTER 1: A HEALTHY DIET FOR SUCCESS

to maintain a professional attitude around the office, no matter what types of adverse challenges or issues hit the fan unexpectedly. Let your supervisors and managers see that you have all the right characteristics of leadership and the ability to work well under pressure.

Another thing that I have found to be an absolute plus in the eyes of upper management is having "excellent" written and oral communications skills.

When you are in any type of customer service setting, what you say and how you say it are equally important. Using slang terminology or speaking to a customer the way that you would speak to a close friend cannot work in concert with one another. A customer can very easily feel like they were not handled in a professional manner, if the company representative does not speak to them in a professional tone of voice and carry themselves with a professional demeanor.

You should always speak to people in a clear, concise, and accurate manner in an effort to get your point across. No matter what industry you are in, communication is the back-bone of everything we do in society. There's no way around it.

With respect to written communications, you should always strive to be well-rounded in this area as well. Depending on what you say in writing, and how you say it, written communication in any form can either work *for you* or work *against you*. Believe it or not, saying anything in written communication form while on the job can easily be a matter of your words or expressions being public record; able to be recalled and scrutinized at anytime for any reason. When the members of the upper management team at your place of employment see for themselves that you have what it takes to communicate accurate, clear, and concise information, you begin to strengthen your credibility and gain leverage in your position that may lead to greater opportunities.

In many cases, employees that are able to demonstrate good oral and written communication skills stand a greater chance of being considered for more rewarding positions within their organization. On the flip side, these same rewarding positions are sometimes given to the people who clearly do not deserve them, but we will dive deeper into this theory in the forthcoming chapters ahead. No matter what the corporate climate appears to be in your workplace, challenge yourself to do the things that you've honestly never done before, so that you may honestly receive the things in life that you've never had before.

If you have dreams and goals of pursuing things that you have an absolute passion for, yet you can't find the time to pursue them due to a demanding work schedule or social life, re-evaluate the things in your life that might be wasting your time.

If your goal is to write a book, but you have no free time after work to get your writing done, try to get the majority of your writing done at work during your scheduled break times. When I wrote my first book, 80 to 90 percent of my writing was done on my lunch breaks over the course of about 16 months. This allowed me to make the best use of my time and get a substantial amount of writing completed.

If your goal is to pursue a college education and earn a degree, but you're too tired to study once you get home, take

CHAPTER 1: A HEALTHY DIET FOR SUCCESS

your homework to work with you and work on it during your lunch hour. Every possible window of downtime that you can take advantage of to complete a personal goal is time well spent.

If you would like to pursue a career in acting, but your work schedule doesn't allow you the opportunity to always be readily available go out on casting calls or auditions, use your PTO (Paid Time Off) wisely and pursue those goals on your time off from work—so that you can at least be putting some irons in the fire and waiting on callbacks from the casting agencies. This is time off that you have earned the right to use as you wish, so take advantage of it!

If you feel the need to get back in shape, make up in your mind that you will cook fresh and healthier foods at home instead of going out for fast food so often. If a healthier diet is your goal that you are committed to trying to reach, then fast food is a poison to you in the pursuit of reaching your goal. Keep in mind what I stated earlier in this chapter—the *goal* is the actual target that you are trying to hit on your road to success; the *game-plan* is the actual process that you will have to follow in order to reach that goal.

If you want to feed your appetite for success, stop doing what you've always done and yet expecting a different result! If you are a car enthusiast who loves fast, exotic cars, put down the *Car & Driver* magazine for a change and pick up *Success Magazine*. After all…what types of people do you think read or subscribe to *Success Magazine*? You're right… successful people! Start reading magazine publications such as: *Network Marketing Lifestyles, Forbes, Smart Money, Fortune, Entrepreneur,* and *Black*

Enterprise, just to name a few.

Taking it a few steps further, there are also some very healthy books that I would encourage you to read, which were written by best-selling author John C. Maxwell: *Failing Forward* and *Developing the Leader Within You*. <u>**Constantly feed your brain the information you want it to retain.**</u> When your brain is constantly being fed positive information, only positive results can start to show up in your life.

If you would like to see some meaningful growth in your personal life and in your career, stop spending so much time telling everyone else how to better their lives and start working more on bettering your own life *first*. Personal growth is just what it sounds like…it's *"personal."* If someone asks you for your phone number or your home address, more than likely, you would tell them that information is personal. In other words, it's none of their business because you don't want them to have that degree of information about you.

The same concept applies when you are in pursuit of personal or spiritual growth. If you waste your time making someone else's problems your priority, then you will never be in a position to visualize your own success. Personal growth is a time set aside to focus on YOU…to evaluate where YOU are in life…to find innovative and effective ways to make YOU a better person for YOU. For a laundry-list of reasons, time is the most precious commodity that we all have as human beings. Use it wisely, or sit back and watch life pass you by. The choice is yours!

CHAPTER 2

Today's Peer Pressures & How to Cope

Though the information in this chapter may prove to be helpful for adults who are over the age of twenty-one, my objective is to reach out to the younger generation to help them better understand the various forms in which peer pressure can present itself in their lives. The goal of this chapter, in general, is to guide you towards a better understanding of how peer pressure affects overall human behavior, offering up some helpful tips on how to cope with various levels of peer pressure and stress as well. Peer pressure is a characteristic of everyday life that has been around since even biblical times, and is a part of life that will always be present in some form or fashion. It is an adverse challenge of everyday living that has the ability to follow us around from childhood well into the latter stages of adulthood.

When it comes to the effects of peer pressure, there is no discrimination! Peer pressure does not care what social class you belong to, how educated you are, how old or how young you are, how fancy your home is, how expensive your car is, what ethnic background you come from, nor does peer pressure take into consideration your religious or moral beliefs. Peer pressure is a lot like death…every human being will experience it at one time or another.

No matter what age we reach in life, peer pressure affects us all in different ways for different reasons. Back when I was a small child, I really did not understand what peer pressure was all about. Looking back, now that I'm older and wiser, I went along with the crowd in most situations because I wanted so badly to "fit in." Fitting in, for me, was a very costly endeavor for both me *and* my parents.

Coming from a very religious upbringing, public schools were a lot harder for me when it came to behavioral issues. At that time, my parents were not on the greatest of terms and, little did I know, the things that went on at home oftentimes adversely affected my behavior at school.

I acted out at school because I felt as though I was not getting enough attention at home and, because of what was going on at home, I was too young to truly articulate to others how things at home were making me feel. Whenever I *did* get attention at home, the attention I got from my mother was far more accepting than the attention I got from an oftentimes bitter, angry father.

Nevertheless, the tension in the house was on a level so much greater than what I could have ever understood. This caused me to be rebellious towards my parents, as well as my teachers at school. From what I remember about most of my childhood, times were remarkably different *then* from what they are *today*.

CHAPTER 2: TODAY'S PEER PRESSURE & HOW TO COPE

A flat screen television was unheard of back in those days. It was all about the HUGE, floor model television that had no remote control to it. If you wanted to change the channel, you had to walk up to the TV and turn the dial (with the proper amount of force…or pliers) to the desired channel you wanted to watch. Then, once you found your favorite program, you had to adjust the two antennas on top of the TV to make the picture come in clearly.

This was back in the day when entire families actually sat down at the dinner table and ate dinner together, while talking to each other and making sure things were going the way they should be. This was back in the day when there was no such thing as cellular phones and TV's in the headrests of cars. This was back in the day when there was no such thing as microwaving your dinner. Dinner was freshly cooked every night, and leftovers were common.

This was way back in the day when the internet was not even *anyone's* imagination yet. I'm talking about way back in the day when kids actually had respect for adults, and were afraid of the punishment they might receive as a result of making decisions that they knew were wrong. Fast forwarding to the twenty-first century, things at home and in the workplace are nothing remotely even close to what they used to be way back in the day! Back in the day, it was an acceptable expectation and standard that men were the primary providers and highest paid earners of the family, while the women stayed at home to raise the children or took on jobs that offered less pay.

Due to technological advancements, and new methods of how companies are now doing business, women are just as sought after in the workplace today as men have been in times past. The simple things in life that were once upon a time the daily norm, in most households, are long gone in today's society.

Sitting down every night to eat a quality dinner with your family and embracing quality time? Are you kidding me? There is hardly any quality time spent amongst family members these days. Everyone is far too busy. Very seldom do you hear about families sitting down at home to enjoy dinner together on a regular basis. Sitting down at home to have dinner as a family has a multitude of benefits.

This is a time where the atmosphere surrounding the dinner event can be controlled. Families can have a nice dinner in the comfort of their own home without worrying about the loud noises and distractions that can be present when going out to a public place to eat. It is also a time where the family can discuss important issues involving how each other's day went, challenges in the home/work/school, etc., or even *solutions* to other challenges that the family may be going through.

No matter if it is within the comforts of home or out in public at a local eatery, it breaks my heart to see families go out to dinner, only to sit at the dinner table together where it appears that everyone is disconnected, doing their own thing and not being engaged with one another. When children sit at a dinner table with their family, and they are allowed to play hand-held video games or video games on a cell phone or other device, I believe *that* is the fault of the parent(s).

CHAPTER 2: TODAY'S PEER PRESSURE & HOW TO COPE

When you are sitting at a dinner table with your loved ones and you are pre-occupied with being on your cell phone, you are sending a very strong message to everyone else at the table that says, "I do not want to be here with you!" Your body language and behavior is suggesting, "I do not want to participate or be included in what everyone else at the table is talking about." These are only a few practical examples of how the evolution of technology has managed to disrupt the foundational integrity of *communication* within the family.

The restaurant industry as a whole, has taken its toll on replacing quality family time during dinner hours. Due to much higher career demands these days, parents are too busy to go home and cook a healthy, hot meal for their families after: working 8 to 10 hour days, dealing with ungodly traffic conditions on long commutes, and possibly rushing home to complete class assignments if they are working *and* going to school.

That's hard enough to get done with two parents running a household. Can you imagine that being the daily routine for a single parent?

Think back to your favorite movie or television program that you couldn't wait to rush home and watch with your family. Just take a good look around you... we as a society are even too busy to sit at home long enough to have a decent family night and watch a few good movies with our kids or family members. We now have the technology to be able to watch television right from the comfort of our vehicles.

This is an essential of everyday living that has even compromised how safe we are able to drive while out on the road. While we should be focused on the roads and reaching our destination safely, we are watching movies in our cars and, in a lot of cases, even allow our kids to playing video games rather loudly while traveling in the car.

Human expectations and standards, coupled with the advances in technology, have replaced how we live our lives. This is the fine line that defines the things that take us over the edge of being content with who we are and what we already have, versus who we wish we could be and what we wish we could have. At the end of the day, we can only be who we genuinely are within ourselves, even if we try our absolute hardest to be someone that we know we're not.

No matter what challenges or hardships find their way into your life, do not let peer pressure overwhelm you and cause you to be someone other than who God intended for you to be.

If God wanted you to be six feet tall and able to slam dunk a basketball, He would have built you that way and blessed you with those abilities. If God wanted you to have a 7,000 square foot home on a hillside, overlooking the ocean, then He would have already blessed you to have that. If it was in God's plan for your life that you would be driving around in a nice, luxury car, then you wouldn't have to feel pressured into obtaining it because you'd already have it.

If it was in God's plan for your life that you would have $1 Million in the bank, then you would already have it. If you feel that you have been asking for these kinds of material blessings, but seemingly have not been able to attain them yet, just be still! When God feels that you are able to handle blessings of

CHAPTER 2: TODAY'S PEER PRESSURE & HOW TO COPE

this magnitude, without letting them control you, then He will unleash these blessings into your life at the right time so that you can enjoy them while keeping in mind how you *truly* obtained them.

CHAPTER 3

Get Over Yourself

Have you ever had the experience of being in the presence of someone who always feels the need to talk about themselves during the majority of a conversation? Have you ever had the nerve-wrecking displeasure of listening to an individual *constantly* reminding you of how much money they paid for some type of material possession?

Can you ever recall a moment in time when you wanted to offer someone a helpful suggestion or recommendation, only to remind yourself that the person you wanted to suggest it to knows everything already? Several years ago, based on these very types of scenarios, I took it upon myself to invent a method that I call the **Flat-Out Approach (FOA)**.

Back when I was a teenager attending the Deputy Explorer Academy with the Los Angeles County Sheriff's Department, my drill instructors taught me that *communication* is referred to as the backbone of law enforcement—and in everything else that we do in everyday life. I am persuaded to believe that, in most social settings, the average individual is capable of communicating with others in a cordial and rational capacity. The manner in which we _choose_ to communicate with others is typically a mirrored reflection of what our overall personality characteristics are made up of.

There are people in this world who don't speak to be understood, they speak to prove that they can talk. There are people in this world who don't necessarily speak to be the voice of reason, they simply speak because they enjoy hearing the sound of their own voice. These are oftentimes the people who have not yet mastered the concept that suggests there is a time and a place for everything and, sometimes when they decide to open up their mouth for the sake of being heard, it is neither the time nor the place! This is when the FOA comes into play.

No matter how hard you may try to overlook the way a person behaves, or how a person's negative comments towards you might affect you, sometimes you have to pull a person to the side and flat out tell them that what they're saying or what they're doing is wrong... flat out! This is a prime example of the **F**lat **O**ut **A**pproach. In most cases, this is something that only a true leader will do. A real leader will be honorable enough to pull you aside and tell you what you NEED to hear, not what you WANT to hear.

I have always believed that, in order to solve problems, you can't beat around the bush and tell people what you think they want to hear. I believe that in order to solve any problem you may be having with an individual, or a group of people in an organization, you must be willing to tell them what they need to hear. Although speaking your mind does fall into the "Freedom

CHAPTER 3: GET OVER YOURSELF

of Speech" category, as a leader or someone who strives to become a leader, it is extremely important to remember that there is an effective and ineffective way to go about being heard.

As in most of the real life applications that I try to describe in my writings, I am going to paint a few pictures in this chapter and, by the time I am finished painting, you will have hopefully learned a few different ways that you can both learn how to get over yourself as well as learn how to empower others to get over themselves, without actually having to tell them to get over themselves in such a harsh or demeaning manner.

Back in the early to mid 90's, I was introduced to a guy by a mutual friend of ours. For the sake of putting this guy on "Front Street," I will just refer to him as "John."

Until recently, John and I had become close friends and we pretty much did everything together within our circle of other mutual friends and extended family members. Camping trips, boating activities, and holiday parties were the norm.

As the years wore on and I began to learn more about John, I started to see a side of him that I honestly did not care for. John was self-employed and blessed to have had the kind of business that was consistently showing signs of growth. With the growth of John's business ventures, also came the growth of his head and his ego!

Weeks, sometimes months, would pass before I saw John at the next function or get-together. However, when I did finally see him, he was not shy about telling me about his new house he closed escrow on and how much it cost him. John was not shy about telling me about the custom-built speed boat he was having made and how much it was going to cost him. If anyone else in my circle of friends or associates had obtained something material that was of any value to them, John always felt the need to get something bigger and better just so that, once he got it, he could brag about it and announce it to the world.

His bragging sessions were never along the lines of, "Look what God blessed me with," they were always along the lines of, "Look what I got! Look what I did!" Really, John? Get over yourself!

When people find their way into my life, by one means or another, they ultimately find themselves being escorted right back out of my life when they start carrying themselves in the ways in which John carried himself. As I got a little bit older, wiser, and more mature, I discovered that people like John had too much of the negative and self-centered energy that I *chose* not to be a part of any longer. I *chose* to start surrounding myself with people who had only positive energy to spill over into my life. I *chose* to start surrounding myself with only the types of professional people who already possessed the values and qualities of the person I was still striving to become.

If you hang out with self-centered, stuck up people on a regular enough basis, you stand a greater chance of developing the same types of characteristics that you don't like to see in other people. With that in mind, be very careful about the types of people that you **choose** to associate yourself with. They can have a greater impact on your life than you can possibly imagine.

In some way, shape or form, we all like to think highly of ourselves. For those who may not understand the basic concepts of how a business organization is structured, it is important to

CHAPTER 3: GET OVER YOURSELF

understand that there is a pecking order, commonly referred to as a chain of command, in every organization. This element of an organization is essential because it ensures that the Standard Operating Procedures (SOP) of the organization will be followed by all employees at all times.

Following or not following the SOP's within many organizations can very easily be the difference between standing in line at the cafeteria at work to purchase your lunch, or standing in line at the unemployment office while wishing you had followed the SOP's.

Maybe you work in an educational setting and you have a distinguished position with a school district. Maybe you are in law enforcement and you've attained a high-ranking position within the upper ranks of your agency. Maybe you work in the medical field and you have finally worked your way up to a highly respected position such as Doctor or Nurse. Now we will take a look at some hypothetical scenarios that work in concert with the career fields mentioned above, and we will make some real-world applications as to how we can successfully empower others to get over themselves.

For the first scenario, we will explore the law enforcement perspective of how department policies and procedures should most commonly be followed. Although this scenario will include more than one individual, your challenge in evaluating this situation will be to determine which person needs to get over themselves the most.

A veteran deputy of the Sheriff's Department comes into work to discover that he will have a trainee riding with him on patrol. When the trainee reports to the station for duty, the training deputy is angry at the fact that the trainee is a female. On a personal level, this particular training deputy feels that being a peace officer is not a career field that is cut out for women. Because he has had more time and experience on the department, the training deputy makes up in his mind that he's going to give this new trainee the ride of her life, as he gives her a crash-course in patrol tactics. For the sake of this scenario, we will refer to the training deputy as Deputy Dummy and the female trainee as Deputy Jensen.

    Approximately three hours before the end of watch, Deputy Dummy notices a vehicle that failed to stop at a stop sign in a residential area. After Deputy Dummy advises Deputy Jensen to get on the radio and call in the vehicle's license plate number for wants and warrants, Deputy Dummy immediately activates his overhead lights and attempts to pull the car over, when he should have waited for a response back from dispatch to confirm if the vehicle had any wants or warrants.

    Deputy Dummy observes the vehicle pick up speed in an attempt to flee, so he advises Deputy Jensen to get on the radio and put out a broadcast, indicating he is in pursuit of a vehicle that is failing to yield. Going by what she learned in the academy, Deputy Jensen notices that the suspect is entering the jurisdiction of another agency and asks Deputy Dummy if she should get on the radio and advise the dispatcher to notify authorities in the next city that a pursuit is coming their way. Deputy Dummy advises Deputy Jensen to stay off the radio, for the time being, because he grew up in that area when he was a

CHAPTER 3: GET OVER YOURSELF

kid and he thinks he knows where the suspect is headed.

While monitoring this pursuit, the Watch Commander advises Deputy Dummy to terminate the pursuit because the suspect has reached speeds too dangerous to continue pursuing him through residential areas. The Watch Commander also advises Deputy Dummy to back off the chase because there is an air unit above who is following the suspect's vehicle at a safer and more tactical advantage. Ignoring a direct order and taking matters into his own hands, Deputy Dummy tells Deputy Jensen that he's going to make the Watch Commander proud by capturing the fleeing suspect on his own, because nobody gets away on *his* watch!

Deputy Jensen admonishes Deputy Dummy that they should heed the direct orders of the Watch Commander and abort the pursuit. Deputy Dummy lashes out at the trainee, stating, "Look! I'm the trainer and you're the trainee, so you do what you're told to do—when you're told to do it!"

The suspect and his accomplice were ultimately taken into custody a short time later, but not before Deputy Dummy's patrol vehicle was hit by multiple rounds of gunfire, fired by the front seat passenger of the fleeing suspect vehicle and, not to mention, a blown out front tire that was also shot out by one of the suspects.

This training deputy was so gung-ho about proving that he was the Big Bad Training Officer who does not back down from *anything* or *anyone* - for *any* reason. He was hell-bent on capturing *his* man, even if it meant putting innocent lives at risk in the community. After a thorough investigation and review of the pursuit by Internal Affairs, Deputy Dummy was permanently relieved of his duties as a result of his reckless actions.

Although it was a noble decision of the department to permanently relieve this officer of his duties, this scenario serves as a scary reminder that there are just as many peace officers still out there who care more about serving their egos more than they care about serving the community. Regardless of the community in which these officers may serve, these are the types of law enforcement personnel that the world can do without.

An officer who displays this type of willingness to put the safety of innocent people at risk is in no mental position to perform his or her duties in a way that would benefit the public. Furthermore, the higher ranking officers within the department, who have more experience and knowledge of how peace officers ought to conduct themselves, should have seen this type of behavior coming from Deputy Dummy long before it materialized to the point of jeopardizing public safety.

You need to realize that, no matter what career field you desire to get yourself into, there will always be people in positions above you that are going to try to persuade you to go against the grain, just because you're new to the company or to the organization. Going against the grain might consist of taking an hour and a half lunch break when you know you're only supposed to take an hour lunch break.

Going against the grain might consist of periodically clocking in at 8:30AM when you know your shift is supposed to start promptly at 8:00AM. Going against the grain might

CHAPTER 3: GET OVER YOURSELF

involve you calling ahead to your office to ask your supervisor or co-worker to clock you in as *"on time,"* even though you're not physically at the office yet because you're stuck in heavy traffic. At times, you might even find yourself compromising what you know is right, just to fit in and be accepted by others.

By doing this, you are also compromising your integrity and even the preservation of your job! In most cases, participating in any of the examples just given above can be the fastest way to lose both your job and your reputation, if you are caught doing either one of them.

When you start a new job or enter into a new career field, your primary objective during your probationary period should be to let your employer see what a hard worker you are. Do not find yourself always going out of your way to brag about yourself so that other people will know how great you are. If you just focus on fulfilling the minimum requirements and job duties that your particular job calls for, let the *quality* of your work speak for itself.

When you can get yourself to the point in your career that your work speaks for itself, you will not have to open up your mouth to ask anyone for better opportunities to grow within the company... opportunities will come looking for YOU!

By the ways in which you do your job, prove to your management team that you have the ability to lead. By the ways in which you lead and tackle your daily responsibilities, you are proving to your management team that the quality of your work contains a high level of self-discipline and integrity. Integrity has already been mentioned in this chapter so, whatever job tasks you are given, always perform those job tasks with the highest degree of integrity. Integrity means doing the right thing, even when no one else is looking.

By using the scenario and example above as a blueprint to YOUR success, understand that there is a Deputy Dummy in every company, organization and career field. The lesson to be learned from this scenarios is quite simple, don't be a Deputy Dummy. "Deputy Dummy, get over yourself! Everyone else has."

Just as civil servants and large corporations are held to high standards of accountability, small businesses are also held to a relatively high standard of accountability as well. For this next scenario, let's now turn the focus on family restaurant supervisor, Audrey Goldberg.

Audrey Goldberg works as a supervisor for her family-owned restaurant, "The Golden Platter." The Golden Platter is a 4th generation, family-owned restaurant that has blossomed into a multi-million dollar empire over the course of several decades.

Audrey's daily responsibilities include: making sure that all employees are properly scheduled for their respective shifts, making sure that all food supply orders are filled and scheduled for prompt delivery, making sure that the restaurant stations are clean and well-kept, and also making sure that all employee time cards are submitted to the payroll administrator on time.

At first glance, Audrey is a very savvy business-minded woman who is always conservatively dressed, drives a decent car and has never really been a materialistic person. Along with the rest of her family members, Audrey grew up going to church for most of her life. She has always believed in treating others as she wanted to be treated. She has always been a very giving person with a kind spirit.

In her free time, she often volunteers at her church by handing out free pancake breakfasts to homeless people in the community where she and her family worship. After several years of Audrey doing all of these admirable things in her community, she began to attract more people into her life and, by doing so, more and more customers appeared to be gravitating to the family restaurant in the form of new business. By far, the family business was turning profits so consistently that the family was entertaining the idea of opening up new restaurants in neighboring counties. Though business was definitely booming, there were some things going on behind the scenes that the restaurant patrons were oblivious to for quite some time.

Since Audrey was the supervisor for the family business, her once mild-mannered, soft-spoken way of leading her staff soon began to take a turn for the worse. Several employees at The Golden Platter were talking amongst each other after their shift one evening. The employees were in agreement that the tips they had been getting appeared to be drastically less than what they had been accustomed to getting in times past.

Just a few weeks after this meeting of the minds, even more employees began to notice a shortage in the tips *they* were getting at the end of *their* shifts. Martha, a waitress who had been with the restaurant for more than two years, came into the restaurant one evening to cover a night shift for a co-worker that needed the day off to care for her sick child.

During the last two hours before the restaurant was due to close, Martha noticed that there was an entire section of tables in the rear dining area that had dirty dishes still on the tables. While standing on the opposite side of the dining hall, taking a customer's order, Martha noticed that Audrey had walked over into the rear dining area and started cleaning off the tables, occasionally putting something into her pockets as she cleared off the tables. As Martha walked into the kitchen area to give the cooks her customer's order, she stood watching Audrey from afar.

It was at this time that Martha could observe that, not only was Audrey clearing off the dirty tables, she was also taking the tip money off of the tables and putting it into *her* pockets. Although she ultimately put the tip money into the huge tip jar where all the waiters and waitresses would put their tips into, Audrey purposely pocketed some of the employees' tips before *finally* putting the remaining cash into the tip jar.

Shortly after witnessing Audrey stealing tip money from her employees, Martha began to notice other things about Audrey that no one else was picking up on. Martha noticed that the once conservatively dressed, soft-spoken, church-going Audrey was now driving a brand new, black Volvo with flashy, expensive rims on it. She also noticed that Audrey was no longer showing up to work in her usual restaurant attire. Audrey was now showing up to work with bedazzled, designer jeans and hats that she was wearing along with the company polo shirt bearing the name of the restaurant.

Martha also couldn't help but notice that Audrey was coming in to work and bragging about how much she paid for

CHAPTER 3: GET OVER YOURSELF

her designer purses and blinged-out watches to accent her new, unauthorized work attire. Since it was Audrey's parents who made the decision to make her the shift supervisor, they did not question her nor hold her accountable for changing her flashy appearance while working in the restaurant.

By this time, all of the employees at The Golden Platter have been made aware that Audrey was seen stealing cash tips off of the dining tables, and they were devising a plan to turn her in.

One night after the restaurant was closed, several employees approached the restaurant owners, Audrey's parents, and stated that they needed to bring an urgent matter to their attention. After having a brief meeting with several members of the staff, the owners admonished the staff that they would look into the matter and investigate it. When Audrey's parents called her into the office to inform her of the allegations that had been brought to their attention, Audrey adamantly denied all of the accusations. She immediately became defensive and told her parents that the other staff members were just jealous of her because none of THEM had been chosen for the Shift Supervisor position.

Since Audrey's parents were so preoccupied with trying to open up new restaurant locations, the investigation into her stealing tips from the waiters and waitresses did not last very long and, quite frankly, was not looked into with any measurable degree of thoroughness or integrity.

Since Audrey did not receive the type of punishment from her parents that all of the other staff members thought she was going to receive, Audrey continued to casually take tip money from the workers from time to time. In fact, Audrey was so angry and so bitter that the employees had gone to her parents and accused her, that she began to become increasingly heartless when she stole money from them again.

Once she found out the names of her accusers, Audrey cut some of their work hours, fired one person, and began bullying several of the other workers. Little did Audrey know, there was one worker in particular who had gone to consult an attorney to see if there was any legal action that could be taken against Audrey for stealing the tip money, and also against the restaurant owners for knowing that it happened but did not do anything about it.

Benjamin, one of the night shift waiters who was aware of Audrey's thievery, was the one who went to have a legal consultation with an attorney to see if the attorney would take on his case and represent him, if the attorney found just cause for prosecution.

Late one evening, while just playing a hunch to test the validity of Benjamin's accusations, the attorney, Sarah Winslow, asked a male friend of hers to join her for dinner at The Golden Platter restaurant. After enjoying her dinner, Sarah encountered the shift supervisor, Audrey Goldberg.

Once Sarah identified who Audrey was, she kept a very close eye on her as she continued to move about the restaurant. Low and behold, just as Benjamin had stated during his initial consultation at the law office, Sarah observed Audrey cleaning off tables in a rear dining area.

CHAPTER 3: GET OVER YOURSELF

She further observed Audrey taking cash tips off of the tables and putting them into her pants pockets, while putting other cash in the front pockets of her apron. Sarah then saw Audrey place the cash from her apron pockets into the large tip jar, but she did not see Audrey remove the cash from her pants pockets. As far as Sarah was concerned, Benjamin's claims were validated and Sarah's law firm soon began drafting legal papers to file a lawsuit against The Golden Platter restaurant and against Audrey Goldberg as an individual.

Now that the staff was aware that Benjamin had an open case against Audrey and the restaurant owners, the other staff members who were affected by Audrey's crime spree soon came forward as witnesses for Benjamin in the legal action filed by the law office.

Once the word spread around town that the restaurant was being sued, and that Audrey was included as a defendant in the lawsuit, Audrey was looked down upon when she began to show her face at her own church that she had been a part of for so many years. Her actions brought shame upon her family members, and also upon the church where she grew up as a small child.

The people who once looked up to Audrey as being a faithful member of the church now looked upon her with an ample level of distrust, and no longer held her in high esteem. The lawsuit against The Golden Platter restaurant was so huge, that the owners ended up settling the case out of court for $980,000.00. Patrons who had once been loyal customers of the restaurant, soon became hard to find. The restaurant that was once booming with vitality and success, was now slowly starting to become a ghost-town.

Within a period of less than two years, the restaurant owners ultimately made a decision to close down the restaurant because business had gotten so slow, it was more cost-effective to just close down and try to rebuild the business at a later time.

In this chapter, the lessons that can be learned by the acts and consequences of both Deputy Dummy and Audrey Goldberg, can most definitely stand the test of time and never become too old to take into consideration.

Deputy Dummy was so stuck on himself that he never envisioned that he would ever be held accountable for his actions, because he was a peace officer who had the power of wearing a badge and a gun. In *his* mind, he was above the law and could handle situations according to *his* own way of doing things, rather than according to the standard and guidelines of the law. Because Deputy Dummy had become so comfortable with being a rogue deputy, he never thought that his actions would ever cause him to lose his dream job of being a Deputy Sheriff, until his unacceptable and inexcusable actions caused him to lose his dream job of being a Deputy Sheriff!

Since Audrey Goldberg's parents owned a thriving and very successful restaurant business, she had the same attitude towards *her* job duties as Deputy Dummy. Once she started seeing the business become more and more profitable, she got greedy because of her love of money and, ultimately, her greed and her criminal acts caused her parents to lose their restaurant business.

CHAPTER 3: GET OVER YOURSELF

Audrey's parents spent over two decades to make their restaurant business as successful as it had become and, because of her self-serving attitude and malicious ways, it only took Audrey less than six months to bring the family business to its knees!

Let the outcome of these two scenarios be a lesson to *you* that, no matter what social class you come from, no matter what fancy title you hold at the company you work for, no matter how much seniority you have at your job, no matter if you work for a Fortune 500 company or a mom and pop, family-owned business, no matter if you have a master's degree or only a high school diploma, your *attitude* towards your daily responsibilities at your job can either negatively or positively define who you really are as a person.

In many career fields, there are some job titles that appear to give some employees a sense of entitlement and power... so they think. There are those who come to work each day to do their job based on the guidelines of their job description and, on the other hand, there are others who come to work each day to abuse their power and authority that comes with the position that they hold in the company.

As you continue on your journey towards success, in whatever organization that compliments your passions, always try to position yourself to be a leader in that organization. Great opportunities are all about *"positioning"* and *"timing."* A good leader always has the keen ability to identify other good leaders in an organization.

If you have a desire to be recognized as a leader in your organization, all you really have to do is follow the steps and recommendations that I have already provided to you in the previous paragraphs. Do your job each day in such a way that, when the quality of everyone's work is called into question, the quality of *your work* can be found to be efficient and completed, done with obvious signs of integrity and dignity. It really doesn't get any harder than that, unless you make it harder than it ought to be.

Position yourself by developing a reputation of always doing great work and, at the right time, you will be propositioned to step into a leadership role sooner than you may think. Remember, your *attitude* towards your daily responsibilities at your job can either negatively or positively define who you really are as an employee.

Whatever tasks you are given at your job or in your organization, always try to tackle those tasks with a positive attitude so that the positive results of your efforts can follow. Just because you are pursuing *your* objectives with a positive attitude, do not set the unrealistic expectation for yourself that you will be pursuing those objectives with like-minded people who are just as positive as you are.

There are a handful of rotten apples in <u>every</u> organization, and there's just no getting around that! Rotten apples within an organization are simply those people who have no obvious desire to follow the rules, policies or procedures set forth by the company or by the organization. People who are labeled as rotten apples are all about doing what *they* want to do, when

CHAPTER 3: GET OVER YOURSELF

they want to do it, and the way that *they* want to get it done... if they get it done at all! These are the types of people in the organization who can mess things up for everyone who is always doing what they are supposed to be doing.

Oftentimes when harsh or more strict policies are rolled out within the company or organization, it's usually because the people who are rotten apples have failed to do something that is an essential requirement, and the company or organization is beginning to see that those actions are negatively impacting their bottom line.

At some point and time, you will encounter situations where you are seemingly the only one working hard on a project or task to meet a departmental goal, yet everyone else around you appears to be goofing off on a daily basis and not ever showing a genuine concern to do their work.

Do not let the childish or unprofessional actions of others around you prevent you from doing what you know is going to speak to the integrity of the work that YOU are doing for the company or the organization. This is when you have to let your work speak for itself... and for you! When you show up to work every day and make a habit of doing great, quality work, you do not have to always *tell* your supervisors or managers what a great job you are doing—they will begin to see it for themselves.

If you find that you are working harder and harder each day to advance within your organization, but the management team is giving greater opportunities to the people who are less qualified, or not doing their work as efficiently as you are, do not panic. People in management who conduct themselves like this are not usually a part of the management team for very long and, once they have been uprooted from their position, that window of opportunity will be available to you once again.

Sometimes you have to just wait it out and allow the people who are rotten apples in your organization to continue wrapping rope around their own necks until, one day, their actions will have caused them to hang themselves—and either be fired or forced to resign. When you want or desire something bad enough, sometimes the hardest part in obtaining it is "being still" until it is the right time for the opportunity to manifest and be laid at your feet.

It doesn't matter if you are a young adult entering the workforce for the very first time, or if you are a seasoned employee with a long-standing work history. You owe it to yourself to conduct yourself in a professional and ethical manner at all times, doing whatever is required of you—performing your job duties with integrity and a sense of dignity. It may not sound like it, simply by reading these words from this book but, in due time, you will see for yourself that following these recommendations will take you very far in life.

Always do your job in such a way that your actions will speak for you. Do not allow the love of money (greed) and the compulsive, obsessive need for power to be the driving force behind your goals and aspirations in life. When you allow your *actions* and your *work ethic* to speak for you, you will eventually start to see that you will not have to work as hard to chase down bigger and better opportunities. Bigger and better opportunities will chase YOU!

CHAPTER 4

How to Identify Your Passions

At first glance, you might prematurely conclude that, judging by the title of this chapter, identifying your passions is an easy task. Well, I'm going to go into transparency mode right now by telling you that, from my own personal experiences, it's not quite as easy as you may think. Gifts and talents will oftentimes have strong similarities so, depending on what you are comparing them to, they might not be so easy to identify at first glance.

In order to help you identify your passions, I have come up with a 3-step process that will help to empower you and motivate you to recognize *your* truest passions. Before diving right into the process, I'd like to invite you to awaken your inner-child and take a walk with me…back down memory lane.

For just a moment, take your mind back to when you were just a child and you were in grade school. Think about all of the things you *liked* about school but, on the other hand, also think about all of the things you did *not* like about school. Think about the teachers that you could easily identify as being your favorite teacher, but also try to call to remembrance the teachers that you wished would go on a long vacation and never come back. Think about all of the cool kids in your class that you always wanted to sit next to in class so that you would have someone to goof around with. Think about the fun games or activities that you looked forward to playing out on the playground at recess time. For the first time in a long time, activate the most vivid memories that you can recall about being a kid...and just live in that moment for a little while.

Where was your family living at that time? Who were your favorite friends to play with in your neighborhood? Where was that one special place that you always looked forward to your parent(s) taking you to so that you could have as much fun as you could stand? What was that one toy that was so special to you that you didn't really want anyone else to play with it? All throughout your childhood, what was the most common question that most adults would always ask you? "What do you want to be when you grow up?" I don't know about you, but I would be a billionaire if I had just one dollar for every adult that asked me that question.

If you were anything like me, no matter how many different adults asked you that question, you wanted to either be a doctor, a policeman, a lawyer, a fireman or a basketball player. Although all of these professions are admirable, children have been conditioned for many years to believe that only *these* types of professions are worthy of trying to obtain. I believe this theory to be true because, in many cases, these children had parents or knew friends of their parents who were already working in these career fields.

CHAPTER 4: HOW TO IDENTIFY YOUR PASSIONS

Therefore, the children who possessed an honest knowledge of what *their* parents did for a living, were directly influenced to start developing ideas on what *they* wanted to pursue as a career once they got older. In this modern day and age, we can now say with every degree of certainty that the theory of yesteryears is no longer true when contemplating the dreams and aspirations of children in today's society.

When you were a kid, you were probably taught the same concepts and principles that the majority of us were also taught. Of the most common lessons that come to mind, you were probably taught that, if you go to school and get a good education, you can eventually get a good job. I am very pro-education, and I believe that having a higher education can definitely carry you very far in life. However, I also believe that having a premier education is not always the determining factor when trying to transition into your desired career field.

Any reasonable person would agree with me when I say that school settings are where we have the greatest opportunities to learn. Not only do we discover the things that we enjoy learning, we also discover the things that we absolutely do not care to learn. It is a journey in our young lives where we learn what we are good at, and we equally learn about the things that we are not so good at. With this in mind, the first step in the process of identifying your passions is to identify your **strengths** and *weaknesses*.

If you are serious about becoming a leader, or becoming a *better* leader, then now is the time to start taking some mental notes and applying these tips that I am going to share with you!

Using a blank sheet of white copy paper, fold the paper in half vertically. Using either a pencil or an ink pen, draw a vertical line down the center of the paper, tracing the inseam of the creased fold—from the top to the bottom. Approximately one to two inches below the top edge of the paper, draw a horizontal line across the page from left to right as shown on the next page.

(See Graph #1).

CHAPTER 4: HOW TO IDENTIFY YOUR PASSIONS

STRENGTHS	WEAKNESSES
1.	1.
2.	2.
3.	3.
4.	4.
5.	5.
6.	6.
7.	7.
8.	8.
9.	9.
10.	10.
(Use the space below to create a new list)	(Use the space below to create a new list)

Graph #1

In the STRENGTHS column, I want you to write down everything that you can think of that you feel you are good at. Write down everything that you feel you have a talent or strong desire to do on a regular basis. Do not limit yourself as to the number of things that you feel can be considered as a strength. Things that you will list in this column are things that you're good at; something that just comes natural for you—or things that you can do very well with very little effort or stress.

In the WEAKNESS column, I want you to write down everything that you feel like you need to improve in your life. Be careful not to be too hard on yourself but, most importantly, be honest with yourself when choosing what things you will add to this column. List the things that you feel you need to work on more. List the skills or abilities that you are not so good at, but you realize you need improvement in those areas.

In most cases, the thing(s) that will ultimately stand out as your true passions will come from your *strengths* column. However, depending on the dynamics of what your overall life-goals are, you just might find that your passion will come from your *weakness* column! Here is an example of why that can end up being a very likely possibility.

If you already see that your *strengths* column is far longer than your *weakness* column, you might decide to challenge yourself one day and pick out one particular weakness at a time and start developing it. If your weakness is math, you may find yourself seeking out math tutorials via YouTube, or even a personal tutor, and learning how to problem-solve more effectively using numbers.

CHAPTER 4: HOW TO IDENTIFY YOUR PASSIONS

If you practice this consistently, and make it a repetitive, disciplined behavior, you may very well decide to move math over to your *strengths* column and, before you know it, you could possibly land a lucrative career as an accountant for a very reputable and well-established accounting firm one day for a prestigious financial institution. By simply changing your mindset, you have the absolute ability to change the direction of your life **AND** change the *quality* of your life in the process! The second step that I want to enlighten you about is identifying your **gifts** and **talents**.

Although they sound like they are one in the same, gifts and talents can have a distinguishable difference between the two, yet still be similar in *concept*. In just a few moments, I will use myself as an example so that you can get a better understanding as to the slight differences between *gifts* and *talents*. A true *gift* is an attribute or character trait about you that is God-given; you were born with it. A *gift* is not something that you can learn how to be good at; you're good at it or you're not. A *gift* is something that other people have to try really hard at accomplishing but, for *you*, it just comes naturally and with no effort. A *talent* is something that can easily be identified as something that you have practiced over a given period of time or something that you have been taught to do.

Here are some examples of **gifts**: knowing how to play a musical instrument by ear without knowing how to read sheet music; knowing how to sing in angelic fashion without ever taking voice lessons; knowing how to draw free-hand, simply by looking at an object one time—or just seeing the object with your mind's eye; knowing how to paint pictures that sell for millions of dollars, and not being able to explain how you did it; having accurate, textbook knowledge about a vast array of subject-matters, without ever having to really study to obtain the knowledge.

Here are some examples of *talents*: becoming a star player on an NBA or NFL team; becoming a successful music producer; becoming an iconic fashion designer; becoming a successful film-maker or building turbo engines for military fighter planes.

Ever since the young age of seven or eight, I have always loved to sing. It didn't matter what kind of songs I was singing at that time, if I knew the words to the song, I could always be found singing. Whenever my mother would take my sister and I on road trips to visit with my grandparents during the summer, my sister and I found ourselves singing almost every song that came on the radio. Not only did we take back-seat karaoke to the next level, we oftentimes took our mother's migraine headaches to the next level as well—as she was trying to concentrate on driving and getting us to our destination safely.

As I got older, my love for singing continued to grow. Once I became old enough to do so, I joined the youth choir at my church and enjoyed singing spiritual songs with my friends from church. After graduating from high school, I auditioned to be the fourth member of an R&B signing group back in the early 90's, pursuing a career as a professional singer/entertainer. Within a few weeks of my audition, I received a phone call from the group's manager, advising me that I was being accepted

CHAPTER 4: HOW TO IDENTIFY YOUR PASSIONS

into the group. We ultimately went on to get signed to Capitol Records and recorded a full-length album.

As time continued to go on, I ultimately became one of several congregational song leaders at my church. I enjoyed leading the entire congregation in our worship services because, for those who know me best, singing *was* and still *is* my way of demonstrating to God how grateful and how thankful I am for the doors that He has opened up in my life! Singing is my way of praying to God, in times when my heart is hurting and just too heavy to even utter the actual words. Singing is simply my way of saying to God, "Father... thank You for continuing to shower my life with Your richest blessings that Heaven has to offer, even at times when I feel so undeserving."

Throughout the many years that I have been singing, people of all types of backgrounds have always asked me, "Where did you learn how to sing so good?" The truth is, I didn't have to *"learn"* how to sing good, singing good was an inborn act that I inherited from birth. Since as far back as I can remember, singing was something that was just a natural part of my family history. All throughout my childhood, my grandmother always told my sister and I about the fact that mega-star Tina Turner was our second cousin from my grandmother's side of the family.

As if having an iconic entertainer in our family was not enough, my father was also a musician. He was a very good saxophone player in the band he was a part of when I was a young boy. Not long after she graduated from high school, my older sister started her own business—which involved people hiring her to sing weddings and special events.

Oftentimes when my sister was hired to sing in someone's wedding, I would sing alongside her and perform duets with her. She kept the money most of the times but, for me, it was just fun to be there with her because it also gave me an opportunity to be doing something that I loved to do. Singing was not the only thing I had a talent for; I also discovered my talent for *writing* at a very early age.

I am not sure if an official study was ever conducted on this theory, but I have always been told that most people are good in either math or in English… they are not typically good in *both* subjects. In my own personal experiences, I have to assume that this theory has merit because I cannot stand math! Math has **never** been one of my stronger subjects, but English and I have been best friends for many years.

Going back to the admonishment at the beginning of this chapter, keep in mind that *gifts* and *talents* can oftentimes have very strong similarities, yet still be somewhat different, depending on a wide variety of variables.

When all of the other kids in my neighborhood were outside playing and riding their bikes, my mother had me sitting at the kitchen table practicing my writing. She did not play, when it came to my sister and I staying on top of our homework and studies. She always had some type of writing assignment up her sleeve for me to work on, in an effort to improve my writing. There were times when the writing exercise would focus on helping me to spell things correctly but, in other instances, the purpose of the writing exercise was to help me to understand what I was writing—so that it would also make

CHAPTER 4: HOW TO IDENTIFY YOUR PASSIONS

sense to whoever was going to be reading what I had written.

Having to be stuck inside of the house at times, when I really wanted to be outside playing with my friends, made me mad quite a bit. It felt like I was being punished for something that I didn't do.

As a kid that really didn't understand why my mother did things the way she did, I began to feel like my mother was just being mean. I didn't quite understand why she wasn't allowing me to do what the other kids were able to do. As time progressed, I slowly started to see that the *way* in which she was making me do things was actually for my good! She was hard on me because she loved me enough to want to see me succeed and, because she was the one that God put in charge of nurturing me and grooming me, she knew it was her duty and her obligation to continue investing in me… even when I wasn't wise enough to see that I was the one who was going to be able to benefit from the *return*!

Little did I know, back then, the stage was being set for the direction that my writing would take for the rest of my life. Because of my mother's diligence, and her mandatory standard for taking my education very seriously, my ability to write grew stronger and stronger. I now see my writing ability as both a talent and a gift.

Since I didn't have a choice as to whether or not I wanted to sit at that kitchen table and practice my reading and my writing, I learned the importance of being able to read and write at a very impressionable age.

The more compliments and accolades that I would receive from people who had a chance to read things that I had written, the more passionate I became about wanting to pursue a career in writing. Not only did I become more passionate about my writing, those compliments and words of encouragement gave me hope...they gave me confidence...they gave me the ability to overcome my doubts—with regard to being able to be competitive as I was entering into the literary marketplace to compete against more established authors, in an effort to make a name for myself.

As my hunger for success continued to grow and my level of writing experience continued to soar, I started to notice amazing opportunities being placed at my feet.

Somewhere between 1997 and 1998, a good friend of mine, who was also a poetry author, convinced me to turn my poems into framed artwork expressions to carry in her store that she owned. Once I saw that the general public was starting to show an interest in purchasing my framed artwork, I became even more empowered and began to solicit other stores to carry my artwork as well. In January of 1999, my framed artwork was accepted into a local Hallmark store. It was a HUGE blessing to discover that MY framed artwork expressions had been accepted into the #1 greeting card store on the planet!

I cannot begin to tell you how good and how accomplished I felt when I walked into that same Hallmark store a month later and, as soon as I opened up the front doors, saw a beautiful display table set up with Valentine's Day accessories surrounding my framed artwork expressions! That was the day

CHAPTER 4: HOW TO IDENTIFY YOUR PASSIONS

when I felt like I had proven to myself, and to the world, that I have what it takes to compete with the best of the best. I have that innovative, competitive edge to show the general public that my work was just as relevant as authors who were far more established and experienced than me. During the summer of 1999, while stepping out on faith to pursue a solo music career, I landed an original song that I wrote onto a compilation album that was released on an independent record label. The first single released off of that album, *"Freak With Me"* (performed by female rap artist Tee Kee), initially hit the Billboard charts at #49 and ultimately climbed up to the #19 position. Although *my* single was never released off of the compilation album, it was still a great accomplishment—knowing that I was even selected to be featured on the front cover of the CD with other talented artists that believed enough in me to want me to be on the album with them.

In May of 2000, I self-published my very first poetry book which was entitled, *"True Inspirations—A Poetry Collection, Vol. I."* The reason why this book release was such a proud moment in my life is because writing that book allowed me to <u>*finally*</u> purge myself of painful and hurtful feelings that were attached to dark and depressing memories that I carried around for decades! Writing that book was extremely therapeutic for me on so many different levels, and it also gave me an unforeseen opportunity to develop my love and my passion for writing.

In 2011, I wrote and self-published my second book entitled, *"No Longer Silent—By Way of Poetry."* Since I knew that I would one day want to try my hand at writing a full-length novel, I used *No Longer Silent—By Way of Poetry* as my platform to get some good practice with discovering the pros and cons of how to make my dream of writing a novel a tangible reality.

Speaking of my dream of writing, I think it's imperative, at this very moment in the chapter, to remind you to *never* stop dreaming! The moment that you stop dreaming, you might as well start planning your own psychological funeral because your *carnal* future is about to die!

When you stop dreaming about the possibilities of accomplishing all of the goals that you've always wanted to achieve, you are literally making a willful and deliberate decision to kill your own future. It doesn't matter what age you are in life right now, it's never too late to dream! It doesn't matter how many things in life you feel that you've already failed at, it's never too late to dream. It doesn't matter that you do not own your own home yet, it's never too late to dream. It doesn't matter that you are not currently driving that exotic sports car that you've always wanted, it's never too late to dream. It makes no difference that, after all of the hard work you've put in over the years, you still haven't landed that leading role in a blockbuster movie, it is never too late to dream!

Although singing came naturally for me, and I went on to become more and more talented in my abilities, never in a million years did I ever think that I would be signed to a major record label as a professional recording artist at just 21 years old... but I never stopped dreaming! Never in a million years did I ever think I would see MY picture on an album cover in Billboard Magazine, but I did... because I never stopped

CHAPTER 4: HOW TO IDENTIFY YOUR PASSIONS

dreaming! Never in a million years did I ever think I would share the stage with LEGENDS such as The O'Jays and The Whispers, but I did… because I never stopped dreaming.

No matter how many times life knocks you down; no matter how badly the dark storms in your life may toss you around and cause you to feel like help is nowhere in sight; no matter how many people turn their back on you when you need someone to lean on for moral and spiritual support; no matter how many times you get looked over for that promotion on your job; I don't care how many people suddenly and maliciously emerge and come against you to attack your character or slander your name, YOU keep on believing in yourself—and keep your eyes on the prize! YOU stay focused on the task of recognizing the gifts and the talents that God has given YOU.

Use those talents responsibly and use them for good because, in doing good unto others, good will also be done unto you. If you put negative energy out into the atmosphere, then that negative energy will eventually boomerang and come back into your life. Some people might refer to this process as karma, while others may refer to it as the Law of Attraction. Equally, if you put positive energy out into the atmosphere, then that positive energy has a duty and an obligation to show back up in your life and manifest itself into that same measure of positive energy.

WHEN EVERYONE ELSE AROUND YOU APPEARS TO BE DOING WRONG, *YOU* HAVE TO BE WILLING TO BE STEADFAST AND UNMOVABLE… AND CONFIDENT ENOUGH TO STAND UP FOR WHAT *YOU* KNOW IS RIGHT!

EVEN IF IT MEANS THAT YOU WILL HAVE TO STAND ALONE, NEVER BE AFRAID TO STAND UP AND SPEAK ON WHAT YOU KNOW IS RIGHT! That is when you will discover the true definition of *integrity*. If you are a person who believes in the power of prayer, start making it a consistent habit to ask for discernment.

Discernment is an extremely valuable asset to possess as you navigate through life. It allows you to see circumstances and situations not just with your *human* eye, but with your *spiritual* eye as well. So, with that being said, if you are a believer, in the slightest degree, get into the immediate habit of praying for discernment; when you pray for discernment, you get wisdom; when you get wisdom, you get understanding; when you get understanding, you get clarity and, at the appropriate times, God will permit you to see and identify things in the *Spirit* that the enemy does not ever want you to see! This is the perfect transition into the third and final step of the identity process.

Identify the *strengths*, *gifts* and *talents* that bring you the absolute *greatest* joys! Once you are able to make a list of all the things that bring you the greatest joys, and always give you a feeling of great accomplishment, you will have finally identified your passions. In case you haven't already been able to reach this conclusion on your own, we are living together in a world where hate is on the rise and love seems to be a thing of our distant past!

As a leader, YOU have the ability to change the world... one relationship at a time. Once you feel that your particular talents and gifts have been revealed to you, use your talents to edify and uplift people. Constantly surround yourself with the types of people who will add value to your life rather than devalue every good thing that you stand for.

As you prepare to put to use the three steps that I have shared with you to help you identify your passions, I leave you with this powerful quote found in my very first book, *True Inspirations—A Poetry Collection, Vol. I.*, "The gifted are they that take advantage of the gift… not they that take advantage!"

CHAPTER 5

So What!

"My father left me when I was just a small child, and he was never there for me; he was not an active participant in my life." "From childhood to adulthood, I was raised in foster care because my mother was addicted to drugs and could not care for me." "My ex-wife left me to be with another man, and left me to raise our children on my own." "I feel like every time I take five steps forward, I get knocked three steps back!" "I have been filling out job applications for over three months now, and not one place has called me back for an interview yet!"

Before I move forward and say anything else, let me first offer some clarity and some reassurance on the quotes shown above—and on what I'm getting ready to say next. I truly sympathize with you if you are the one who has a father who was never there for you, and left you to grow up and figure out life all on your own; that is *my* story too. If you should just so happen to fit into the shoes of the person who was raised in foster care because your parent(s) could not care for you and give you a better quality of life, I get it; my heart goes out to you in a real way. If your ex cheated on you with someone else, and it killed what you thought was a promising relationship, I can relate to you, because it happened to me too...TWICE!

These quotations above are among the very hardships and set-backs in your life that can truly cause you to get lost in your emotions and become consumed with the feeling of overwhelming defeat and sadness. This may sound a bit harsh and insensitive at first but, by the time you get to the end of this chapter, you just might thank me for saying it. If you have been unjustly hurt; if you have been wrongfully accused; if you find that you have been loyal in your relationships—to disloyal people; if you feel like you are always being unfairly treated, I'd like to say, from the bottom of my heart...SO WHAT!! Yes... you read that correctly. So what!!

This may very well be one of the hardest things you've ever been asked to do but, for the sake of you gaining some mental and emotional peace in your life, I would like you to sincerely consider accepting what I call, the **SO WHAT Challenge**.

Between the ages of about nine to twenty-seven, I harbored a great deal of hate towards my father and, at times, an occasional expression of resentment towards my mother too. Silently, and internally, I hated my father simply because he was never there for me during the most critical times in life when a young boy or young man needs his father's love... needs his father's reassurance... needs his father's guidance and involvement in his life. Since I didn't have my *actual* father present to help me navigate through life, I was blessed to have influential men take

CHAPTER 5: SO WHAT!

me under their wing to show me the ropes about what becoming a respectable young man was supposed to look like. Although I can now look back and appreciate their value in my upbringing, I was not mature enough back then to truly see the relevance regarding why their involvement in my life was going to prove to be so essential.

A common attribute that all of these influential men had in my life, was that they all knew that I was being raised by a single mother who was doing the best she knew how to do with me. The majority of the men who groomed me into young adulthood were the men within the leadership ranks of my church.

Whenever I would get into ongoing trouble in school, my mother would tell these men what I did at school and, when we got to church, they pulled me aside IMMEDIATELY and checked me for the unacceptable ways in which I was misbehaving in school. They didn't just pull me aside and give me a short peptalk, they reprimanded me as if I were one of their own sons—so that they could show support to my mother who was trying her best to raise me up in the way that they all knew I should go. It was a team effort; it takes a village to raise a child, and they were all a much needed part of my village.

Due to me not knowing how to accept and adjust to the fact that my parents were no longer together, as a young child, I became the American mascot for incorrigible kids around the world who were going through the exact same thing as me.

The more I started to realize that my father wasn't in my life, and that he was not making any noticeable efforts to *be* in my life, that negative emotion of abandonment and rejection turned me into a very angry young boy, and I took that anger well into my young adulthood. There came a time when no one could talk any sense into me; it was MY WAY or the highway! My attitude towards life eventually began to take a toll on my grades as well.

Even though I was grateful and appreciative of the men who were planted into my life to fill the void of having an absent father, I was angry at the world because the man that I WANTED to be in my life was not there. I got tons of moral support and encouragement from the men in my village but, at the end of the day, I didn't get any encouragement from my father. Although I got endless emotional and financial support from the men in my village, I didn't get any from my father.

At some point in life, I ended up seeing for myself that leaving my father was the best thing that my mother could have done for all of us! The resentment that I once held for her went away and I was able to turn that negative energy into something positive.

I can never forget the passion and the desire that I had within me when I wanted to write and publish my very first book. I was so excited that I could not stop talking about it. Once I began the initial writing process, and formatting my outline as to how I wanted my book to look, the overwhelming feeling of satisfaction became my new adrenaline to keep moving forward until I had turned a mere idea into a tangible book.

Then, after a long talk with my mother, reality set in and I was faced with making a life-altering decision! My mother could tell that I was obviously overtaken with a strong sense of pride and excitement as I was just beginning to tackle my goal of writing my first book.

CHAPTER 5: SO WHAT!

In a calm voice and a spirit of motherly humility, she told me that I would never accomplish greatness on the level in which I was pursuing it until I first got rid of the hurt and the anger in my life that I felt towards my father.

She went on to tell me that, if I was not willing to forgive him for the hurt that he had caused, and the abandonment he that he forced me to feel, it would be highly unlikely that I would have a successful future.

I thought to myself, "How much longer am I going to decide to remain angry for all of the things my father never did for me? How many more years am I going to sacrifice being able to move forward in life because I want to continue holding on to my baggage from the past?

After recalling to memory all of the negative things that I can remember about my father, I thought to myself, "SO WHAT! SO WHAT he wasn't there for me… his loss! SO WHAT he never called me to wish me Merry Christmas or Happy Birthday… his loss! SO WHAT that he hasn't called me in nearly 10 years to ask how his grandchildren and I are doing… his loss!"

Once I got good at maintaining that SO WHAT attitude, it became so much easier for me to just completely let go of the things that previously triggered all of those hurtful emotions that made me a bitter and angry person as I was transitioning into adulthood. It was the equivalent of having a huge burden being lifted off of my shoulders, but on a continuous basis. When I followed my mother's advice, bigger and better things began to happen for me.

When my first book was finally published, in May of 2000, I was able to get it placed in a local Borders Bookstore, where the book went on to sell out on four different occasions. The success of that book empowered me to want to write another book, which I did. In 2002, I self-published a children's book entitled *"Mask Man,"* written by an author that I had signed to my publishing company back then. It was just like my mother said; once I had let go of the hurt and anguish of my past, things were really starting to take off in a more positive direction for me.

Continuing on the path that my mother had already told me was ahead of me, I went on to self-publish my second book, *"No Longer Silent—By Way of Poetry,"* and also got that book into the Barnes & Noble distribution system. I cannot possibly begin to describe the sheer happiness and empowerment that comes along with knowing that people are still buying books that I wrote some 8 to 19 years ago. That is the power of earning residual income; doing something ONE TIME and getting paid for it over, and over, and over and over—without having to ever repeat the effort.

Just as I had gotten the hang of implementing that SO WHAT attitude to get over the disappointment of having an absent father, new challenges ultimately surfaced that forced me to lean on that concept even harder!

For the people in my village who are closest to me, it is no secret that I was madly in love with a beautiful woman who was my ***everything***… she was my best friend; she was my all-in-all… she was my one and only true and unconditional love; she was Heaven-sent and came into my life at just the perfect moment— when I truly needed a strong woman standing beside me.

This woman was so special and so adored by me, I always affectionately referred to her as my "Queen." I referred to her

CHAPTER 5: SO WHAT!

as Queen so much, that my kids thought Queen was her real name! It would be untruthful of me to say or suggest that I was not the cause of some things in the relationship that did not go according to what a healthy relationship should be. No matter what challenges came up in our relationship, we were mature enough and honest enough with each other that there was nothing we couldn't work through...so I thought.

In July of 2018, we seemed to be butting heads more frequently than we had been in the past. In my opinion, however, the issues we were having were issues that could have definitely been resolved between the two of us. In the months following the onset of our relationship hurdles, I got the overwhelming feeling that she was cheating on me and, unfortunately for our relationship, I was right!

Although I eventually confronted her with the cheating allegation in November of that same year, I also let her know that I knew she was cheating months before I confronted her...I was just giving her a space of time to see how long it was going to take her to come clean about it and tell me the truth. When I gave her the name of the man that I knew she was cheating with, she denied it for as long as she could hold on to her lies but, in the end, she lost track of the lies she was telling me and had to tell me new lies to cover up the lies that she *could* remember.

Even during the times that things were not always the greatest between us, we still stood in agreement with one another that we loved each other and that we desired to continue moving forward to take our relationship to the next level and get married in 2019.

When we would spend time with each other on weekends, we went to various locations looking for new furniture and accents to decorate our future home. We took my kids and her grandchildren out to dinner and to the movies quite often to let them bond with one another. When her daughter gave birth to her second child, I was there with her on the days she went to visit her daughter in the hospital, and I even held her newborn granddaughter when she was first born.

Whenever Queen came over to visit my children and I, she never had to lift a finger to do ***anything***! I always kept a clean, neat home; I was always in the kitchen cooking for her. When she would come to visit us on the weekends, we oftentimes went out to eat breakfast at our favorite go-to restaurants. It was not unusual for us to stay home while I cooked her scrambled eggs, grits, bacon, smothered potatoes, and whatever choice of beverages she wanted!

When we were not going out to eat at a five-star restaurant, I would stay home and cook dinner for her—baked Salmon, steamed asparagus, home-made garlic mashed potatoes and topped off with a frosty glass of Moet champagne. Just to make her feel like the Queen she once was, I would even do all of the dishes after dinner and completely clean up the kitchen…just so that she could go relax and enjoy the fact that she had a King that loved her enough that he was willing to show her things that she NEVER experienced when she was married!

It was a match made in Heaven, and everything about our relationship seemed so genuine and so promising…until I confronted her with all of the evidence I had complied, which

CHAPTER 5: SO WHAT!

proved she was cheating on me with the same man she was lying about in the beginning when the accusations surfaced.

Words alone are not nearly enough to describe how heartbroken this woman left me when she ultimately admitted to being in another relationship behind my back! After already enduring a sour marriage and a relentless custody battle with my ex-wife, I was ready to give my Queen my hand in marriage for the rest of my life.

On December 1, 2018, I was supposed to be having a surprise proposal party for her but, after much prayer and careful consideration for a healthy future, I just could not go through with spending the rest of my life with a woman who had no shame in lying to me on the level in which she did. Over a decade ago, people telling complete lies about me nearly cost me 50 years to life in prison for something that I was not guilty of so, when it comes to people lying to me, it resurrects a very dark time in my life that had me feeling like I had hit rock-bottom and, based on that past experience, I just cannot tolerate anyone that I'm planning to spend the rest of my life with lying to me like that. If she found it so easy and so conniving to lie to me as a girlfriend, just imagine how much damage she could've done with her lies as my wife, if I had not found out about all of her crooked ways on my own!

Having to let go of this relationship, with someone who was supposed to be my Queen, was undeniably one of the hardest things I've had to do in many years but, nevertheless, it was necessary. I realize that there is no such thing as a perfect relationship, and that people do make mistakes, but what she did to our relationship was a mistake that could not be given another chance to repeat itself.

December of 2018 was the start of a new, yet equally painful, journey for me…much like the one I experienced when I accepted the fact that my father did not wish to be a consistently active part of my life.

This breakup with my ex-girlfriend took a severe emotional toll on me, and I felt as though my happy life, as I once knew it, would never be the same. As people in my village began to surround me with their love, their understanding and their support, once again, I started to have a more grateful disposition about ending my relationship with this woman who was supposed to be my Queen.

I started to see that this break-up was for my own good, and that I should not be allowing it to alter or devalue who I was as a person. At some point, I began to thank God for the fact that He allowed me to see this woman's true colors <u>*before*</u> I put a ring on her finger and trapped myself into being with her for the rest of my life. Just as I had done after previous hardships had devastated my life, I switched my attitude about our break-up back to SO WHAT mode!

Every time I began to feel down or depressed about my circumstances, I began to remind myself, "SO WHAT she cheated on me; it just means that now she has someone new to cheat on because that's who she is! SO WHAT she led me on and tried to have her cake and eat it too; that's just what selfish people do. SO WHAT we don't spend quality time with each other anymore and have long talks on the phone; that's more time that I have to continue chasing *my* dreams! SO WHAT she will never be my wife; that just means that I now have room in my life to allow God to send me the *right* woman who understands and appreciates my value, and will stop at nothing to honor it and preserve it unconditionally.

At this point in the chapter, if all you are focusing on is the fact that I was transparent enough to even disclose the things my ex-girlfriend did to derail our relationship...you are missing the lesson in the testimony.

In order for you to truly grasp the lessons offered throughout this book, you must focus on the lesson, not just the testimony. It is my fervent belief that, in order for us to rebuild our lives on a more solid foundation, we must first be willing to tear ourselves completely down. In order to better position ourselves to start our healing process, we must be willing and fearless about exposing who or what hurt us, but yet transition into solution-mode so that we can move forward in a healthy manner without punishing the person in our future relationships for things that were not their fault; we must hold ourselves accountable for how we hurt people and, at the same time, we must go to that person we hurt and humbly ask them to forgive us for how we have hurt them.

Refusing to go to someone that we have hurt, and ask for their forgiveness, leaves us in an unhealthy position to have greatness become an essential part of our lives.

The next time that these or other adversities may show up in your life, I sincerely hope that you take me up on my **SO WHAT Challenge.**

When you have that SO WHAT attitude during a time in your life when things just don't appear to be going the way you need them to go, you are immediately releasing negative energy that can no longer have a stronghold over your life... unless *you* decide to give it power!

When you take on that SO WHAT attitude towards troubling issues, what you are ultimately saying is, "I don't care anymore! SO WHAT I didn't get accepted into Harvard University; I still have a promising chance at getting accepted into USC! SO WHAT I didn't get approved for that auto loan; God was probably helping me avoid going further into debt. SO WHAT the bank rejected my home loan application to buy a house; my faith tells me that God is about to approve me for something He knows I can better afford. SO WHAT my boss didn't choose *me* for that new position I applied for; I have faith that God is about to bless me with a better job offer with a brand new company! SO WHAT I wasn't able to afford that new Bentley; I'm going down to the dealership next week to pick out a new Porsche!"

The outcome of any negative situation or circumstance is all dependent upon your mindset. If a positive outcome is what you truly desire after a trial or tribulation, then your only choice is to figure out a realistic way to turn that negative into a positive! Doing it any other way is the equivalent of failure or defeat.

Less than two months after I broke up with my ex-girlfriend, I began to take on that SO WHAT attitude towards the demise of our relationship so that I could allow new, more positive blessings to flow into my life.

CHAPTER 5: SO WHAT!

On January 4, 2019 I was blessed with an opportunity to be a keynote speaker at an out-of-state, corporate event...which I gladly accepted. In the days and weeks following *that*, I began to gain more and more positive momentum on completing this book. I could also feel God positioning me to be partnered with the right people to make this book a great success and ensure that it falls into all the right hands of those in our world who are willing to position themselves *today*—so that they can go in search of a more rewarding *tomorrow*... be it on their job or in their personal life.

Once I got blessed with being presented with the opportunity to be a keynote speaker as previously mentioned, I felt like God was using that experience to speak directly into my life! It felt like God Himself was saying to me, "I know she broke your heart, My child, and I know she deceived you and caused you to feel like a failure—but you now have a choice to make. Do you wish to continue focusing on all of the aches, pains and disappointments of your *past*...or do you wish to move forward and focus on all of the other blessings that I am going to continue to lay at your feet?"

This book coming into existence was my answer to that question. At the end of the day, I am glad to share that my ex-girlfriend and I mutually agreed to finally sit down and talk, so that she could give me a sincere apology, in person...and not hide behind her emails and text messages like she had previously done. Forgiving her was the best thing that I could have ever done for my present *and* for my future, and I truly do wish her all the best in her personal and professional endeavors!

The personal experiences that I have just shared with you, in the most transparent way I know how, are clearly not the first nor the last time that things of this nature will happen in life. You will always encounter adversity throughout your lifetime, but how you choose to handle your adversities TODAY plays a critical role in the type of leader you will become TOMORROW!

Once you learn the concepts contained in this book, put them to immediate use and see for yourself —how applying these principles will enhance your personal and professional life. Keep in mind that success isn't for everyone; it's only for the people who have a passion and a burning desire to obtain it. Another thing to remember is that you cannot make payments on success! The price for success is almost always paid in advance, up front! As you may one day strive to empower others to follow you, based on what you've learned, just remember—some will…some won't...but, then again…SO WHAT!

From this day forward, despite the many dark storms and personal hardships you may have had in your life thus far, I highly recommend that you stop focusing on all of the negative hands that life has dealt you—start changing your mindset to believe that you *are* deserving of a greater life than what you've already experienced.

Start speaking **LIFE** into your life! When you start speaking *life* into your life, life happens! When life happens, you start to accomplish things that you never thought you'd be able to achieve. When life happens, you start to notice that God is removing toxic people from your life and replacing them with

CHAPTER 5: SO WHAT!

people of a higher caliber who add value to your life.

When life starts to happen, you're no longer pounding the pavement looking for good jobs…good jobs will start looking for you—because of your positive mindset and your positive energy that you radiate everywhere you go! Once you change your mindset and start speaking *life* into your life, you are no longer wondering how your rent or your mortgage is going to get paid! When life starts to happen, you can finally go shopping for the things that make you feel good—without being concerned about how much it costs.

When your mindset changes and life starts to happen for you, the bad things you did in your past are suddenly overwhelmed by all of the *good* that you are doing NOW! Stop holding yourself hostage in the prison of your mind, and start planting seeds of prosperity in your life, simply by changing the way you think! Having a successful future is a choice. If you choose to keep staring your past in the face, you will never see your future! Choose wisely!

CHAPTER 6

Time Management & Accountability

Accountability is an aspect of leadership that must be taken seriously at all times by anyone that desires to become an effective leader. At some point and time, we have all heard someone say to us, "Don't take it so personal." Well, accountability should be regarded in the exact opposite frame of mind. Holding yourself accountable, and allowing others to hold you accountable as well, is a non-negotiable element of leadership that you have no other choice but to accept and adapt to...and take it very personal.

When you tell someone that you're going to do something either *with* them or *for* them...DO IT! When you tell someone that you are going to call them at a certain time...DO IT! When you tell someone that you are going to be at an event on a specific date...DO IT! If the day should ever come when you don't have as much as $5.00 left to your name, you ALWAYS have your word! Your word is your bond, and it stands on its own merit the moment you make a commitment to carry out a task at a given time. Sometimes doing the smallest things can make the biggest difference.

If you should ever start to develop a reputation for *not* keeping your word then, in actuality, it becomes evident that your word has no value.

As you continue your quest to learn what leadership is all about, and the many dynamics that make up this key leadership ingredient, you will soon find out for yourself that you cannot ever expect people to validate you as a leader if you demonstrate to them that you do not own your flaws and mistakes—and openly lay out strategies that will allow you to improve in those areas where you keep falling short.

Somewhere along your career path, you may find yourself in a position of leadership (management) in which you will be given the power and the authority to discipline an employee.

While looking through the eyes of integrity, you should not punish your subordinate employee(s) for failing to do something that they never see YOU do. If you expect your employees to take care of you, then take care of your employees FIRST. If you want your employees to respect you, then let them be the beneficiaries of you respecting them FIRST! As a leader, every end result begins and ends with your ability to lead effectively.

Accountability is an extremely necessary and essential element that must be acknowledged and implemented at all levels of leadership. If the element of accountability is noticeably missing from your leadership tool box, then you can rest assured that there will not be very many people who will maintain a sincere desire to want to follow you. If you feel like you do not know very much about the importance of accountability, do not allow yourself to develop pitiful excuses for your lack of

CHAPTER 6: TIME MANAGEMENT & ACCOUNTABILITY

knowledge...look it up; research it for yourself until you obtain credible answers. If you can utilize Google to get the answers to other random things that add no value to your life whatsoever, then you can utilize Google to research all of the attributes of leadership. *Time* is the most precious commodity that we all have in this life. Always use your time wisely to seek credible information...which eventually turns into reliable knowledge...which eventually turns into wisdom...which eventually turns into achieving goals.

The next thing I'd like to draw your attention to is the importance of **time management**. Time is very precious so, when it comes to pursuing your goals, pursue those goals with *urgency* and *excitement*! A very critical tool that I always teach people is—plan your work and work your plan! In other words, every goal that you strive to reach should be about planning and execution. Plan the goal, and then execute all of the steps that it is going to take to reach that goal.

Another thing that I want you to get into the habit of doing is physically writing down all of your goals on a sheet of paper and apply a *due date* to each goal. A goal without a due date is not a goal...it is only an idea! An idea without a due date to compel it to become a reality is a complete and utter waste of your time. If there is no action behind your idea, that means there's no urgency or excitement to motivate you to chase the goal. If you are new to this way of doing things, do not write down unrealistic goals on your goal sheet. As you will eventually find out, that will also prove to be a waste of your time.

Just to see how well you will do with achieving your goals, start off by writing down three short-term goals. DO NOT write down on your goal sheet that you want to be a millionaire within six months! It is highly unlikely that you will achieve such a goal within that short period of time.

Once you have achieved the short-term goals, then start over again and write down another three short-term goals that you'd like to achieve. After you have achieved your second round of short-term goals, then start writing down three long-term goals. You cannot possibly be planning goals *and* spending unnecessary time participating in activities that do not push you towards those goals.

One of the most common ways that I see a lot of people wasting valuable time is being on social media 24/7! In my opinion, based on some personal challenges that have come up in my life on two separate occasions, social media is the devil's playground if you're not careful with what you allow yourself to get sucked into!

The way I see it, if you add up the total number of hours that you have spent on social media in the period of one month, you will see a more vivid picture of how much of your valuable time you are LITERALLY wasting away every day!

I have a few quick questions for you to really, honestly think about and answer honestly…don't fool yourself. What is the greatest satisfaction that you get when you are posting on social media for hours and hours within a day? Who are you trying to attract with what you are always posting? Are you posting for the purpose of seeing how fast people respond to your posts? Are you posting things simply to see who will stand in agreement with you, by indicating that they either "Like" your post...love your post...think your post is funny or if they are angry at what you posted?

Are you simply bored out of your skull, and that's why you are on social media posting almost every hour on the hour? What is the real reason? Do you have something to prove to society by what you are posting? Are you seeking validation from a specific person or group of individuals who may want to RSVP to the pity parties you keep inviting everyone to? Are you lonely and just need attention? Do you feel rejected by society and subsequently seek constant validation by social media shenanigans? Do you have a job?

If you are the type of person who can easily be considered a social media junkie by the amount of time you spend posting all of your business online, yet you find that you answered "No" to the last question I posed above, there is something terribly wrong with your life! How are you okay with spending more time on social media than looking for a job to earn a living to take care of your responsibilities? If what I said doesn't fit your current situation, then you're not the one I'm speaking to. However, if what I said *does* fit your current situation, you really do need to get a grip on your life before it is everlasting too late!

Stop tricking yourself and brain-washing yourself into believing that you have time to get your life in order, because tomorrow is not promised to any of us. You can't keep saying to yourself, "I'll start applying for jobs next Monday," or, "As soon as I pay off the balance of my back taxes I owe, then I'm going to start working on building my business next year." What? You're going to start applying for jobs _next_ Monday? You're going to start building your business _next_ year? For real? That's how you roll?

It is that very form of thinking and mindset that has you stuck in your life right now, right where you are! Because you are a prisoner of your own mind, psychologically, you don't even realize that you're free to think on a higher level than what you've already been doing! You are holding yourself hostage when you continue to think the way you currently think. If you want to free that hostage within you, you have to start thinking outside of the box in all areas of your life. Speak life into your life and life will happen for you. If you are a believer, then prayer is one of the most powerful things you can start getting good at FIRST! I am living proof that there is power in prayer.

If it were not for a multitude of people who prayed over my life nearly 15 years ago, I'd be sitting in prison for life right this very second—for something I was never guilty of doing! Oh, but God! Through the power of prayer, God kept me in the palms of His unchanging hands and delivered me from the front porch of hell. If He saw fit to do that for ME, how much more do you think He can do for you? All you have to do is hold onto your faith and you will be utterly amazed at what He can bring you through.

I could have been gone a very long time ago, but I have now accepted the fact that the reason why I'm still here is because God has a divine purpose for my life. Find your purpose in your life for why you think God still has you here on the _time_ side of life. Find your passions in life that bring you happiness and joy.

CHAPTER 6: TIME MANAGEMENT & ACCOUNTABILITY

Pray for God to grant you clarity on understanding where He needs you to be.

Whatever you do, DO NOT PRAY FOR PATIENCE! It is extremely risky to pray for patience because, when you pray for patience, what you are really asking for is more trials and tribulations to come into your life! Without obtaining even more trials and tribulations after praying for patience, how else will you be able to measure if you have acquired patience or not?

When you pray for patience, more heartaches and pains must come into your life to test your level of patience. Rather than pray for patience, pray for discernment. I cannot stress this enough; when you pray for discernment, you get wisdom. When you get wisdom, you get understanding. When you get understanding, you get clarity. Once you get clarity…you now can see where God wants you to go and what He needs you to be doing.

Once you come to have a mature level of discernment, God will oftentimes allow you to see things in the Spirit that the devil never intended for you to see or find out. And another thing… let me make something perfectly clear to you—you don't have tomorrow, you only have RIGHT NOW! You don't have until next Monday to start that diet you've been talking about for years, you only have RIGHT NOW! You don't have until next month to start loving your kids more, you only have RIGHT NOW! You don't have 90 days to start becoming a better leader, you only have RIGHT NOW! You don't have until January of next year to become more giving towards people, you…only… have…RIGHT… NOW!

I have always been amazed by the fact that most of us will quickly stand in agreement that tomorrow is not promised to any of us, yet we are constantly telling other people what we will be doing days and weeks from now. If you were raised in the church as I was, you grew up being reminded that the Lord comes like a thief in the night. When I was much younger, I didn't quite understand those words the way I thought I did, but now I get it.

When thieves appear in your life, their objective is to steal the most valuable things that you own. If someone approached you and told you that they have concrete information about a thief who is planning to break in your house next Friday night, wouldn't you be planning on being home that night so that you can be ready to stop the thief? A thief is not going to voluntarily tell you when they are going to break into your house to steal from you so, in essence, it only makes sense that you stay ready at all times so that you are prepared to defend what is rightfully yours.

Instead of wasting your precious time on routinely doing things that add no real value to your life, push yourself to do things that bring you prosperity; push yourself to do things that bring you to develop and maintain a stronger spiritual walk in whatever your faith or religious beliefs may be; push yourself to be a better servant to others who have greater needs than you may have; push yourself to be about the business of uplifting and edifying others to strive for greatness, and let them know that you are willing to walk beside them on their journey to help them in any way that you possibly can.

CHAPTER 6: TIME MANAGEMENT & ACCOUNTABILITY

I see so many people on social media posting photo after photo of themselves having fun while traveling to exciting places, doing exciting things with their friends and family members and also participating in exhilarating activities and just appearing to be free from all of life's woes. In one or more of these types of photos, I will usually see a caption that says, "Living my best life!" That sounds like a very promising and persuasive metaphor to use in a social media post, but oftentimes it is a smoke-screen to prevent others from seeing into your life the things that you are trying to mask or forget about.

If you were truly living your best life, would you even have that much time to be on social media all day, every day? If you were truly living your best life, would you really have the time to post your every move on social media? Since it is the goal of this book to encourage you to start thinking outside the box more frequently, I want you to consider this philosophy. For each and every time that you find yourself saying that you are living your best life, what you are actually saying is, "This is probably as good as my life is ever going to get, based on how sad of a journey it's been so far." Saying that you're living your best life could also be taken as you saying, "I am really happy in this place where life has me right now and, since this feeling may not last very long, I might as well live it up until this moment finally dies out."

When you speak out into the universe in this fashion, what you're really doing is telling the universe that this is the greatest life that you desire to live and that you do not need life to grant you anything greater than what you're already experiencing.

Speak life into your life, and watch life happen for you in ways you never even imagined. Don't cut off your blessings by entertaining negative thoughts, negative speech or surrounding yourself with negative people.

Whenever I am doing live interviews or keynote speaking events, I get very passionate about encouraging people to "speak life into their life." When you speak life into your life… life happens! It may not always happen when you want it to, or the way you want it to, but you will experience a blessing, nevertheless. Everything that you say or think activates the Laws of Attraction. If you speak negative words or think negative thoughts, a negative outcome occurs. If you speak positive words or think positive thoughts…a positive outcome occurs. As much as you can possibly remember to do it, speak and think only positive things so that positive outcomes can show up and overwhelm your life in ways that you never thought were possible!

Unless they admit this fact to you directly, you would never know that most people who are always filled with laughter, and fun-loving silliness, and hilarious jokes to tell, are actually doing those things to mask some type of deeply-rooted hurt that they are feeling within them. I know this to be true because, for many years, I have found myself masking my emotional flesh-wounds by making other people laugh!

For me, being silly from time to time and making other people laugh was my way of escaping the hurt and emotional anguish that I had once kept bottled up inside of me. There were times when my tribulations were just so burdensome to

CHAPTER 6: TIME MANAGEMENT & ACCOUNTABILITY

carry, I just wished that I could wake up in a place where no one knew me. I was so heavy-hearted with one thing or another, I didn't want to think; I didn't want to talk; I didn't want to be a listening ear for someone else; I didn't want to get up and dust myself off and keep trying; I didn't want to care; I didn't want to hear advice from anyone...I just wanted to be left alone in those moments.

To be painfully honest with you...there were times when I wanted nothing more than to just give up! For some odd reason, I guess it was never in God's plan to allow me to quit or just flat-out give up. The more and more I thought about giving up, the more and more I thought about my kids. What would my kids think if they ever found out that I quit at something? What kind of message would I be sending to my kids if they ever saw me give up on myself? I couldn't take that chance, so succeeding at the tasks before me continues to be my only option. When you're trying to raise leaders, you never teach them or show them how to quit...you teach them and show them how to overcome and WIN!

One of these days, when we least expect it, the Lord is going to come to pay us a visit just like that thief in the night...and we need to be ready to meet Him. Remember when you were a kid and you used to play hide and seek? The very last thing you said out loud when you were finished counting was, "Ready or not...here I come!" That's how I oftentimes think that God will come for us that way, when He's ready. Do not take this day for granted, thinking that you have the rest of your life ahead of you. That all sounds good for everyday conversation but, realistically speaking, none of us really have the rest of our life ahead of us...we just like to *think* that we do, because we have hope. We must always have a realistic mindset to live each day as if it were our last day because, in reality, it just might be.

CHAPTER 7

Knock It Off

Think back to a time in your life when you said to someone, or someone said to you, "Knock it off!" It may have been decades ago, or it may have been just yesterday but, at some point in your life, you have had to tell someone to knock it off.

Whether I'm trying to motivate and empower a large group of people, or if I'm simply trying to mentor and empower an individual, there is one realistic principle that I try to teach as I'm grooming someone for leadership or personal development. In order to fully understand the dynamics of what makes people do the things they do, you must first identify and understand the things that *YOU* are capable of doing as well! In order to truly be in a position to teach others about themselves, you must also know and understand the dynamics of your own personal life—and be able to identify whether or not *your* character traits also work against you, or if they complement your character and work in your favor.

I honestly thought long and hard about offering my apologies for the things that I am going to say in this chapter, but then I came to my senses! I immediately began to think to myself, "Why should I apologize for taking time out of my life to write a book that teaches people how to become a more powerful and amazing version of themselves?" So, having said that…there will be no apologies! At some time or another, we've all had to swallow a few tablespoons of *pride* and *tough love*; this is such a time.

You cannot realistically expect to go through life always having things go your way. You cannot realistically expect to go your whole career without having to deal with salty co-workers and bosses who will eventually get on your nerves for one reason or another. You cannot realistically expect to go to work each day expecting that your supervisors and managers are always going to be empathetic towards what you are going through, be it in your personal life or your professional life.

One of two things is going to happen between now and the end of this chapter. Either you're going to see your reflection in the forthcoming scenarios—*and* do something to change your life for the better, *or*, you're going to break the mirror and turn a blind eye to the things that you know you can do a better job at, but yet you refuse to see a need to change…which makes you a questionable leader, at best.

Whatever position you choose will be proven not by what you *say*, but by what you *do*. **Leadership** is an <u>action</u> word, so failure to take the appropriate actions to lead your life or your organization in a positive and healthy direction truly calls into question your ability to lead.

A true leader is only a leader based on who is willing to follow them. If you consider yourself a true leader, yet you question if there is anyone out there willing to follow you, it might be a good idea for you re-evaluate what you feel makes you such a great leader.

Leadership is also an *attitude*! If you consider yourself the leader in a personal relationship, then your *attitude* towards your relationship can largely influence whether or not that relationship is going to be a happy, healthy one—or a bitter, destructive one. If you are already in a leadership position in your current career field, then your *attitude* towards your staff and towards your job responsibilities can one day become the determining factor as to if you keep your leadership position or not. If you are a community leader, then your *attitude* towards how you will lead and safeguard the citizens in your community can play a detrimental role in deciding if you will be re-elected for another term, or if you are voted out due to your inability to lead, based on the community's standards. If you are a pastor or other leader within your church, then you should already know what is expected of you, by God's standards, and how you are being charged to lead, as outlined in the scriptures.

Have you ever been so out of it that someone literally had to smack you upside the head to get your attention and force you to focus? Have you ever had to splash cold water on your face to wake up your senses just enough to be able to get your day started? Well, this chapter will be that smack upside the head to get your attention…and that ice cold splash of water in your face to wake you up to confront your realities!

Respectfully, the goal of this chapter is to challenge you to *own* the type of leader you are today, and focus on areas that you feel can use a leadership make-over. If you are one of those people who feel like you have what it takes to become a leader that others can look up to and respect, then the goal of this chapter is to challenge you to examine your imperfections more closely so that the *truest* leader within you can finally emerge!

In most companies and organizations, there is a leadership hierarchy or management structure, which some people also refer to as a "pecking order." A hierarchy, or pecking order, is an organizational structure that allows you to see *who* in the organization is above *who*. When you initially get hired for a new job, you will typically report to a specific <u>lead</u> person, or <u>supervisor</u>, who will decide what your initial workload is going to be. They will also be responsible for monitoring the production and overall quality of your work, to evaluate your work performance and possibly to help you stream-line areas within your workload where you might be able to improve your efficiency.

Your supervisor most commonly reports directly to your department <u>manager</u>. The manager's job is to ensure that the supervisor and the lead are making sure that all other employees are working diligently on the work assignments that they have each been given. Depending on the nature of your company or organization, your manager will oftentimes report to either a <u>director</u> or a <u>project manager</u>. If you are not sure about the management structure or hierarchy within your company, ask your immediate lead or supervisor to assist you with how to obtain that information.

CHAPTER 7: KNOCK IT OFF!

The reason that I'm giving you this basic knowledge on how to identify corporate management structures is so that you can have a better understanding of various roles within your company or organization. In order for any company or organization to have the greatest chances at being successful, it is extremely vital that each person in the company or organization understands their role, and how their role can positively or adversely impact the organization's bottom line.

Whenever there is a major shift within a company or organization, that shift almost always starts within the very top positions and works its way down into less prominent positions in the organization. Having had the experience of being a part of the management structure for companies that I have worked for in the past, I wholeheartedly believe that leadership starts at the **TOP** of *any* company or organization! I was the type of leader that refused to discipline my staff for something they did wrong—if I was the one who failed to show them how to do it correctly. The most effective way I was able to be a leader to my staff members is that I led by example. If I was expecting all of my staff to have their shoes shined and their uniforms cleaned and pressed, then I showed up to work with MY shoes shined and MY uniform cleaned and pressed.

If I expected my staff to treat the general public with dignity and respect, then I allowed my staff to see ME treat the general public with dignity and respect. The bottom line is simple, when you're a true leader, you always make it a point to treat people with the same level of professionalism and respect that you wish to receive from them.

If you are someone's supervisor, stop trying to discipline your employees for arriving late to work, when you yourself are rarely ever on time! If you are someone's manager or project manager, stop complaining that your subordinate management staff never gets their reports to you on time—when you are not giving them the right tools and resources they need to do their job more efficiently! You cannot expect to win a modern day war with ancient, defective weapons! Stop expecting your staff to produce high quality, 21st Century work—with pre-historic software and office equipment! To say the least, that is a very unrealistic expectation to have. If you want your employees to produce better work, give them better tools to *do* their work.

Now that I feel like I have your attention, it's about time to take a more modern day approach in getting you to truly understand the type of leader you are today, and how you can improve to become an even better leader tomorrow. Following my sincere beliefs that leadership starts at the top of any group or organization of people, I'm going to start with the "alleged" leaders that are currently over the top of all of us, and I'm going to show you how a person's inability to lead can adversely affect an entire nation of people.

DISCLAIMER: ON BEHALF OF ALL OF THOSE WHO SHARE THESE VIEWS, THE FOLLOWING STATEMENTS ARE CONCERNING THE INDIVIDUAL WHO IS UNFORTUNATELY, CURRENTLY RUNNING OUR COUNTRY.

I cannot begin to tell you how disappointed and heart-broken I am with the current administration of our country,

CHAPTER 7: KNOCK IT OFF!

and the way in which Mr. Trump is leading our nation. I find it extremely difficult to even refer to him as President because everything that makes him who he is does not appear to be indicative of how a sitting President ought to be acting in the public eye. Aside from the many other distasteful things about him that I could focus on, that he has either done or failed to do, my empathy and my compassion for my fellow American cannot turn a blind eye to the many families who have suffered and been harshly affected by his childish and tacky decision to move forward with a partial government shutdown.

Because of his partial shutdown of the government, scores of people across our country went to bed at night wondering if they would live to see the next day because they could no longer afford to pay for costly medication that was helping them to sustain life. So many families stood in emotional and psychological torment, wondering if they would still be able to feed their families because they no longer had a paycheck coming in. Because of this government shutdown, children across our country were sent to school hungry because their parents were no longer able to afford the extra snacks and lunch foods that they were once able to send their kids off to school with. In some cases, parents had no extra money to give their kids to buy a lunch at school. As much as I love children, this broke my heart into pieces. It broke my heart to see that Mr. Trump's infantile temper-tantrums were more important to him than his consideration of how his decision to shut down the government was going to punish EVERY American, not just the government workers. If this is the kind of leader *you* are, and you know it…KNOCK IT OFF!!

If your style of leadership is the type of leadership that sends kids to bed hungry and prevents parents from bringing home a paycheck to take care of their families, then KNOCK IT OFF!! If you call yourself a leader and you feel like people *not* being able to afford life-saving medicine is no big deal, then that's not leadership…that's a SINKING SHIP!

Since day one of him taking office, Mr. Trump continues to take undeserving credit for the things in our country that "appear to be" going right, but is always refusing to take credit for things in our country that are going absolutely wrong. This is not an example of how to be a leader, it is an example of how to become a cancerous infection in our society.

If you are a leader, and you see nothing wrong with how Mr. Trump treats and disrespects women without shame, then your ethics meter is as wrong as two left shoes! If you see nothing wrong with Mr. Trump's decision to partially shut down the government, then your leadership compass is *completely* broken, and you should not be held in high esteem to hold **ANY** office of honor, profit or trust in our nation!

DISCLAIMER: **If you currently hold a title of lead, supervisor, manager, assistant manager or higher, then this section is your opportunity to reflect on the type of leader you have been, and make the necessary adjustments where they are needed.**

Along my journey of writing this book, I had the pleasure of speaking with a random and diverse variety of individuals about

CHAPTER 7: KNOCK IT OFF!

what it's like to work at their particular places of employment with the management staff that oversees them. In this section of the book is where you managers will get a chance to see a more colorful and realistic picture of what your leadership looks like through the eyes of your subordinate employees. The magnitude of what I am about to say does not just come from my perspective, but it also comes from the perspective of people in your organization who are sick and tired of being treated the way that you sometimes treat them.

It's a new day today, in the hearts and minds of many employees in today's workforce who are no longer willing to just sit back and be quiet about how they are being unfairly treated by people in the management position that you hold. Yes, that *YOU* hold...definitely hold yourself individually accountable and KNOCK IT OFF!!

For so many decades, employees around the globe have witnessed and experienced deplorable and unfair treatment in the workplace. If you fall anywhere within the ranks of management, however slight, you need to know and own the fact that there are some members of your staff that think you are a terrible leader and, in some cases, I am persuaded to believe that they are right. The reason why your staff members don't pull you aside, or come to your office to tell you about yourself, is because they need their job and they're afraid of getting fired if they rub your ego the wrong way!

Rather than come to you directly and tell you what their issues are, they keep it bottled up inside of them because, in their minds, you are not as pleasant or as approachable as you would like people to believe. Another reason why your employees don't bring troubling issues to your attention is because, based on how you have spoken down to them in the past, you have already left them with a lasting impression that makes them feel like you don't even care and that you're not going to do anything to fix the problem!

Why would your employees keep on wasting their time to bring problems or adverse departmental issues to your attention when you didn't do anything to fix the problem(s) the first time they told you about it? KNOCK IT OFF! Here are some modern day management behaviors that will _**definitely**_ cause your staff to look upon you as a lackluster leader:

- Offering overtime opportunities to your favorite employees but not offering it to your entire team.

- Promoting your favorite employees to higher positions just because you like them, not because they're qualified.

- Openly participating in workplace gossip with subordinates who have a reputation for being "messy."

- Allowing your favorite staff members to *purchase their promotion* by always buying you lunch, bringing you breakfast on their way into the office, or buying you your favorite Starbucks drink and running all of your little office errands, as if they are your personal secretary.

- Approving the time off requests of the staff members that you *like*, but denying the requests of other staff members that you don't particularly care for.

CHAPTER 7: KNOCK IT OFF!

- Implementing disciplinary action against the staff members you don't like but, when the company policies are broken by the people you *do* like, you turn a blind eye to anything *they* get caught doing.

- Granting unethical approval for a staff member to go run a personal errand on company time—because he/she is directly related to you, yet not offering that same consideration to other staff members; nepotism.

- Passing out Christmas gifts to only your permanent employees and not giving anything to your team members who are working for you through a temp agency.

- Passing around a birthday card for a staff member in your department, while being careful **_not_** to pass it to the person in your department that you don't want to sign it because you don't like them.

- Warning your staff members about abiding by the company dress code, but yet **_not_** saying anything to the woman in the department who wears tight, short miniskirts and blouses that expose more than a respectable amount of cleavage.

- Constantly insulting the intelligence of your employees by participating in the very departmental conflicts that you ought to be working to resolve, as a real leader would do.

- Showing obvious signs of favoritism towards one race of employees but not the others.

- Failing to own the fact that, if you're not a part of the *solution*, you're a part of the *problem*!

- Discriminating against an employee because they are not of the gender that YOU approve of. Should I continue?

- Walking into the office each morning and picking and choosing which staff members you will say *'Good Morning'* to and which staff members you will completely ignore!

- Failing to respond to work-related emails from the person you're angry at for telling *your* boss that you're mistreating them and behaving unprofessionally towards them.

- Giving dirty looks to the people in the office that you *think* went to HR to complain about you. If you were leading in the way that a true leader would lead, you wouldn't have to worry who went to HR to complain about you—because there would be anything for people to complain about in the first place.

- Failing to discipline the company bullies that have been brought to your attention on numerous occasions by your staff members.

- Allowing other people in the office to hear you telling foul, inappropriate jokes that may be offensive to others.

- Always giving praise and accolades to the employees that you *like*, rather than praising the employees who clearly did all the work that makes YOU shine.

CHAPTER 7: KNOCK IT OFF!

- Finally figuring out the dynamics of a huge departmental problem after several *years*, then expecting your staff members to find a concrete solution to those problems within 7 to 10 business *days*. That is an unrealistic expectation, to say the least.

- Always coming up with departmental goals, but yet never making yourself available to your staff to help them reach the goal(s). You are forever TALKING ABOUT IT, but never BEING ABOUT IT.

- Fooling yourself into believing that, because of your fancy title and your prestigious position in the company, you don't have to be empathetic, compassionate, caring, giving or even courteous to your staff.

- Thinking that you can sexually harass your employees because you think that your fancy, corporate title makes you untouchable and above the law. Harvey Weinstein thought he was untouchable too but, as history continues to prove, you will one day reap what you sow!

- Failing to lead by **example**! If you cannot demonstrate the ongoing ability to lead by example, then you should turn in your leadership card and call it a day!

As a leader, if you are guilty of any of the aforementioned examples of poor leadership mentioned above, I am directly and personally challenging you to search deep within your core values, if there are still some left, to re-define who you truly are as a human being FIRST, and as a leader second. As much as you would like to think you do, you don't know it all! EVERY DAY is training day! Every day is an opportunity to learn something new that you may have never considered before. None of us have *truly* arrived. You must always remember that your staff members are not following you because they think you are a great leader. In most cases, they are following you because they have to! They're following you merely because the organization had already taken its form before they joined the company and had to *tolerate* the leadership that was already in place.

This is that part of the leadership process where the rubber meets the road. This is that part of the leadership process where you have that heart-to-hart conversation with yourself in the mirror and say to yourself, "If progressive growth and productivity in my organization is essential in keeping with our organization's mission statement and core values, then the *attitude* that we will all need to get us there MUST start with me first!"

DISCLAIMER: IF YOU ARE A PARENT, REGARDLESS OF YOUR AGE, THEN THESE MENTORING NUGGETS PROVIDED IN THIS SECTION ARE OFFERED TO YOU IN AN EFFORT TO HELP YOU EITHER BUILD OR STRENGTHEN THE RELATIONSHIP BETWEEN YOU AND YOUR CHILD(REN).

In every family structure, each person in the family has a different role. Before you can try to positively identify the areas in which you can be a better parent, you must first understand your *true* role in your child's life. First and foremost, your children need to understand that they are not your equal; they are not your friend…they are your child!

CHAPTER 7: KNOCK IT OFF!

Too many parents in today's society have abandoned their role as *parent*—to entertain and accept the false reality that their child is their equal, or their *"bestie,"* rather than their son or daughter. WRONG! Your child is your child and, if you don't start operating in your child's life as the parent you were meant to be, your child may never learn to grow up to appreciate the sacrifices, hardships and struggles you went through to get them where they are today.

As a parent, if you have a child that talks back to you on a regular basis, comes in and out of your house as they please, brings other kids in and out of your home that you know nothing about, smokes cigarettes or marijuana, drinks alcohol, back-talks their teachers at school or refuses to respect authority, the problem is not just your child….the problem is YOU!

When I was growing up as a child, there was no such thing in my culture as talking back to an adult! That was the purest form of suicide back then! I grew up during a time in society where, if an adult who knew your family saw you getting into trouble or behaving disrespectfully, it was not unusual for that adult to spank you for being disrespectful. Not only did that adult spank you for your public display of wrong-doing, they would also go to your parents and explain to your parents WHY they had spanked you. Once your parents got you home, they spanked you again for showing out in public and shaming the family that raised you better than what you were demonstrating out in the public eye.

In my home, my sister and I both grew up with having the utmost respect for my parents, especially our mother. As kids, we didn't always agree with having to do the things our parents were telling us to do but, at the end of the day, we did it...and we did it quietly and IMMEDIATELY, because we know what would happen if we did it any other way. Kids nowadays do not seem to be learning much respect in the home. You can always tell when you're out in public and you hear for yourself how kids talk to their parents. Still to this day, I literally cringe when I hear a parent call out to their child and the child responds by saying, "What!!" Are you kidding me? If that was ME saying that to my parents, as a minor child, I would have ran away from home, and then been afraid to ever go back home for fear of having to face my consequences for being disrespectful.

No parent should EVER allow their child respond to them by saying, "What!!" When your child responds to you that way, what they are really saying to you is, "What do you want? You're bothering me!" When you allow your child to talk to you that way at a very early age, during the most impressionable stages of their young lives, what you are really doing is grooming them to be disrespectful towards other adults, and you, as they grow older.

Several years ago, an acquaintance of mine was having difficulty with her adult children. As long as I have been acquainted with this woman, I have been told quite a few stories involving her children speaking to her with a very cold, disrespectful tone of voice. Oftentimes when she would describe incidents to me between her and her children, my response to her would usually be, "They say stuff like that to you? They said it to you exactly how you repeated

CHAPTER 7: KNOCK IT OFF!

it to me just now?" Once she confirmed that this is how her children had been speaking to her, I then asked her, "Why do you allow your *kids* to talk to you so disrespectfully... even though they're young adults?"

Since some of the stories she had told me were similar in nature from when her now adult children were much younger, I asked for her permission to offer her my opinion as to why her adult children were demonstrating this type of behavior. After she gave me permission to offer my opinion, I went on to explain to her that her children had been behaving this way since they were much younger and, now that they are adults, they are only acting towards her how she has allowed them to act towards her for most of their life.

If you don't train your children to respect you during the youngest years of their life, you cannot be shocked or surprised when they grow up to be adults who still have that same level of disrespect towards you as they did when they were young children. That is just an unrealistic expectation, especially in today's society.

As parents, you cannot, by any stretch of the imagination, allow your children to grow up thinking that they are your equal...they're not! You must demand respect and honor from your children at all times. Your children must learn from YOU that they cannot speak to you the way they speak to their peers. Even though I grew up being raised by a single mother, when she spoke on something, there was no further conversation about the matter. What my mother said was the final law, and she was not in the least bit concerned with what I felt about her decision…and that's the way it's supposed to be! From what I continue to see in how children are raised today, it appears as though the roles in the house are being reversed; parents are so busy trying to be their child's friend, and the kids are taking over the house and doing what they want to do, WHEN they want to do it and IF they want to do it.

Your child can either learn respect from YOU at home, or they can learn it from the correctional officers who will be controlling the prison that they end up at if they continue to grow up thinking that they can do whatever they want to do! I do not make this statement with the hopes that your child will one day end up in prison, I make this statement in the reality of knowing that, if your child continues to grow up thinking that they don't have to respect authority, being an inmate in prison can one day become *their* reality. Do not relinquish your parental control over your children…you just might live to regret it, so KNOCK IT OFF!

DISCLAIMER: IF YOU ARE A MINOR CHILD BETWEEN THE AGES OF 13–17 YEARS OLD, OR IF YOU ARE BETWEEN THE AGES OF 18–25, THE INFORMATION CONTAINED IN THIS SECTION IS FOR YOU.

"Who keeps coming into my room and going through my stuff?" "Can you please stay out of my room when I'm not home?" "Who ate the rest of my pizza that was in the refrigerator?" "Why did you think it was okay for you to go into my room and look through my closet?" "Why do I have to be back inside of the house every weekend by 10:00 PM, when all of my other friends are allowed to stay out until midnight?"

CHAPTER 7: KNOCK IT OFF!

If you are under the age of 18 years old and you have made any of the above statements to your parents, you really need to KNOCK IT OFF! If you are over the age of 18 years old, but you are still currently living with your parents—acting like your parents are the ones who live with *you*, then you absolutely need to KNOCK IT OFF!

If you should so happen to forget anything else I have said in this book, remember this…your parents don't owe you ANYTHING, but you owe your parents EVERYTHING. Before you read any further, let that sink into your spirit for a few more moments.

Because you are not a parent yet, your brain is not even mature enough to even begin to understand and appreciate the sacrifices that your parents have made for you to be where you are in life right now. Because everything has been given to you thus far, you have no real idea about what your parents have to put up with at work every day just so that they can earn a paycheck to take care of YOU!

If your parents buy your food, buy your clothes, give you lunch money for school each day, pay for your cell phone bill every month, pay to keep a roof over your head, pay your school tuition, pay the utility bill each month so you can be warm in the winter and cool in the summer, pay for you to participate in sports, pay for summer vacations that you can enjoy, pay for the things in life that you need AND even for some of the things that you want…then you really don't have anything to complain about.

And for the record, that room in your parents' house that you have been referring to as "your room," that is not *your* room...that is your parents' room! If you don't pay the rent or the mortgage, then you are simply sleeping in the guest room... because you are a guest. See how that works? So when you are living in your patents' house, and they ask you or tell you to do something, it is your job to be about the business of doing what is asked of you...WHEN it is asked of you.

Oftentimes when your parents ask or tell you to do something that you don't want to do, you talk back to them and/or question them as to why they are asking you to do it. Life is going to get so much easier for you once you understand and master this concept...your parents don't owe you an explanation for ANYTHING, but you owe your parents an explanation for EVERYTHING! It's called honoring and respecting your parents!

Behaving like this towards your parents only shows them that you do not appreciate all of the things that they have done for you. Behaving like this towards your parents is the perfect way to develop a bad reputation for being ungrateful for the things that people do for you. Once you have developed a bad reputation for being unappreciative and ungrateful, you will start to notice that people will eventually stop doing things to help you because they will already assume that you won't appreciate the help.

As you get older and begin to start to transition into adulthood, you should have already learned the basic responsibilities and survival skills that are going to enable you

CHAPTER 7: KNOCK IT OFF!

to take care of yourself and remain independent. Once you get on your own, it will not take very long for you get a crash-course in experiencing what it's like to be that grown-up you had always wanted to be when you were a child.

In the beginning of your journey as an independent adult, things are going to appear to be very exciting for you. You'll be able to come and go as you please; you'll be able to have friends come and go into your home as you wish; you will be able to host that wild house party you've always dreamed about throwing and you will not have to worry about anyone constantly nagging you to clean up after yourself. However, one of these days, hardships and tribulations are going to find their way to your front door…just like the rest of us.

This will be the day when you will wish you had listened to the wise counsel of those in your inner-circle who tried to teach you things when you didn't want to listen. This will be the day when you will wish you had taken the helpful advice of those who tried to warn you not to continue hanging around unsavory people who are always getting into some type of trouble time and time and time again. This will be the day when you will be faced with the possibility of being homeless because you don't have enough money at the end of the month to pay your rent or mortgage to keep a roof over your head.

Whatever knowledge or wisdom you can learn from your parents, learn it NOW while the blood is still running warm in your veins, because they're not going to be here forever! Whatever valuable lessons that you can possibly learn from your parents, learn as much as you can from them while they are still in their right minds to even be able to teach it to you.

Don't fall into the bad habit of procrastinating to get important things done that will push you closer towards your goals in life. Don't keep fooling yourself into believing that you can wait until next month or next year to start being a better son or daughter. Don't keep fooling yourself into believing that your parents were not hurt by something harsh or disrespectful that you may have done or said to them, when in fact they were very hurt!

I know this might sound a bit scary to receive but, at the end of the day, you don't have TOMORROW to right your wrongs… you only have TODAY! Tomorrow was never promised to any of us so, rather than give your parents a lifetime of heartache and grief, tell them as often as possible that you love and appreciate them for all that they have done for you. Tell your parents daily how thankful you are for the sacrifices that they made to demonstrate their unconditional love for you.

Even if you have a parent that has not been there for you… that has not made any sacrifices to help you get where you're trying to go in life…that has not cared enough about you to remind you how much you are loved each day…there is someone out there that God has placed in your life to fill in the gaps of your life to be a blessing to you. Make it your business to thank God for those types of people in your life each day. Take the time to do these things TODAY because, if you keep on waiting until tomorrow, they are going to pass away and be gone forever…taking with them YOUR opportunity to have told them that you love them—one last time.

CHAPTER 7: KNOCK IT OFF!

<u>DISCLAIMER</u>: IF YOU ARE A TEENAGE BOY, A YOUNG ADULT MALE OR A GROWN MAN, THIS SECTION BELOW IS SPECIFICALLY FOR YOU.

It is painfully obvious that, so far, no one in your life has cared enough about you to call you out by letting you know that CRACK KILLS!! People in society are sick and tired of seeing you guys walking around sagging your pants and showing off the crack of your butt, and your unsightly underwear or boxers! Really? That's how you're going to represent yourself for the rest of your life? If you have a $160.00 pair of tennis shoes, a $900.00 cell phone and a car with 20" rims along with $2,500.00 worth of audio equipment in your car, somebody raised you without teaching you how to prioritize your life!

It amazes me that people spend so much money on things that don't matter, but yet they cannot afford a $12.00 belt to hold up their pants. Simply amazing! For every day that you make a conscious decision to leave your house with your pants almost down to your knees because you think it's sexy to show off the crack of your butt, you have no idea how many potentially great opportunities are passing you by the moment that people in your community lay their eyes on you!

For many years, there has been a long-standing controversy over where sagging pants first originated from. Some people believe that sagging their pants to expose their butt, or their underwear, first began in the prison system as an inmate's way of alerting other prisoners that they were looking for sexual attention from another inmate. Others believe that sagging pants also began in the prison system, but was due to inmates being made to wear prison pants that were too big for them—

and that belts for the prison issued pants were not allowed due to safety or security liabilities. The bottom line is, regardless of where it originated from, purposely sagging your pants like you do makes you look like a totally indecent, uneducated and ignorant fool.

I don't say these things to you to degrade you, but you truly need to know what many people in society think about you when you come out of the house carrying yourself in this manner. If you say you don't care, I don't buy it. What you're most likely feeling inside is that the people closest to you in your life who you feel should've cared more about you may not have cared at all, so that made you angry enough not to care about how you present yourself even more.

Most people are never going to tell you these things about yourself, because they do not want to make you feel bad or provoke a confrontation with you. It makes no sense that they refuse to tell you to pull your pants up simply because they don't want to make you feel bad because, truth is, if you don't care about how this fashion felony makes you look in the eyes of society…you are already, internally (psychologically) feeling bad about yourself! A person who feels good about themselves, and confident about themselves, and who respects themselves, and feels dignified within themselves would NEVER walk around this planet with their pants sagging down to expose the crack of their butt to the world! KNOCK IT OFF!

When you walk around your community sagging your pants like that, you are making very defining statements about yourself that say, "I am sagging my pants because I don't

CHAPTER 7: KNOCK IT OFF!

truly know who I am. I am sagging my pants because I don't recognize my worth or my value. I'm sagging my pants because everyone else is doing it. I am sagging my pants because my favorite rap artists do it in their videos. I'm sagging my pants because, when I was a little kid, I saw my father sagging *his* pants. The reason why I am sagging my pants is because I don't love myself; I don't love myself because I feel like no one else loves me either." If *THIS* is your way of thinking, you are not a leader...you are merely a follower. With this type of negative mindset, you will always be a follower until the day that you decide to change your mindset—so that the lifestyle you truly want begins to follow YOU!

For those of you that are walking around claiming to be thugs, just for the sake of trying to fit in, stop blaming all of your failures in life on the police officers who keep arresting you and hassling you for doing things you have no business doing, and for being in places you have no "legal" business being in. I agree with most, that there are some extremely corrupt police officers in our world. However, I'm persuaded to believe that there are more good cops than bad cops! If you hate the police so much, stop giving them something to do every time they see you hanging around people that you clearly do not fit in with!

It makes me sick to my stomach when I hear people saying that the white man is not giving them good jobs and a better chance at having a better quality of life. To the people who think like that, I say to you, "Who put a gun to your head and told you not to get into a community college or four-year university? Who put a gun to your head and said you cannot pursue a higher education? Who has you hostage to the point where you cannot look for a job or seek a better job to elevate yourself from where you may already be in life?"

Is it the white man's fault that you refuse to be productive? Is it the white man's fault that you choose to hang around people that add no value to your life whatsoever? Is it the white man's fault that you didn't finish high school or get your GED yet?" If you hate the police, stop selling drugs in our communities and they will stop kicking in your front doors at ungodly hours of the night and day! How about THAT? If you hate the police so much, stop walking around with nothing better to do with your life than sag your pants halfway to the ground and hanging around with gang members that you THINK are your friends! How about THAT? If you hate the police so much, make sure you're not stupid enough to have your entire car smelling like weed (marijuana) when they pull you over for a minor traffic violation! How about THAT one?

Stop blaming society for everything that's not going right in YOUR life and start taking a closer look and what YOU are doing to be a part of the very problem that you say you hate! People who practice living law-abiding lives don't have to worry about being mistreated by the police all the time because, since they make more responsible choices than YOU, they don't attract police!

Even though I'm speaking primarily to the young men of our communities, I also want to echo this to everyone. When the police pull you over and give you commands to do something... **PLEASE JUST DO IT!!** I'm telling you this from a very real and

CHAPTER 7: KNOCK IT OFF!

a very personal perspective, based on what I learned many years ago when I was just a young Deputy Explorer Cadet with the Los Angeles County Sheriff's Department. Little do you know, the commands that they give you on a felony traffic stop, or during any other type of investigative detention, are designed to ensure the officer's safety at all times but, more importantly, they are also designed to ensure *your* safety—as long as you are compliant.

If you are getting a ride somewhere by a friend, and you have no idea that the car your friend is driving is stolen (or being used without the owner's consent), you are going to be in for the scare of your life when a patrol car gets behind that car and runs the license plate number! Just so you can know ahead of time what to expect, I'm going to run it all down to you as best as I can:

- When the police run the plate on the car you're riding in, and it comes back as stolen, that officer is going to immediately get on that radio and start requesting additional units at his/her location.

- Once the primary officer sees that he/she has sufficient units to safely attempt to pull that car over, that's when you'll notice a sea of red and blue overhead lights come on…and you should also hear sirens, as this will be considered a felony traffic stop.

- For every minute that you ignore the lights and sirens, and refuse to pull over immediately, you are making an already bad situation extremely worse…and more dangerous than it needs to be.

- If you fail to yield (in other words, if you refuse to pull over), every traffic violation you make during your attempt to elude the officers is being recorded and documented, and will ultimately be used against you in the form of additional charges once you're caught. If you are smart enough to pull over, which I highly recommend, follow their instructions to the letter!

- Once you stop, all of the officers behind you are going to have their guns drawn on you! This is absolutely NOT the time for you to be moving around in the car and reaching under seats or trying to hide what you think is more important than your life. This is the time to be still and wait to hear instructions. At the officer's discretion, you will be ordered to turn the car off (and possibly told to throw your car keys out the window) and get out of the car, at which time you will be told to face away from the officers with your hands straight up in the air. The officer will then tell you, "Walk backwards towards the sound of my voice until I tell you to stop." THIS IS NOT THE TIME TO DROP YOUR HANDS DOWN TO YOUR SIDE OR STOP WALKING BACKWARD SIMLPLY BECAUSE YOU THINK IT'S A BRIGHT IDEA! Doing that might get you severely hurt...or possibly killed if it is believed that you are reaching for a weapon. This is the humiliating part, but you must do it! When the officer feels you are a safe distance away from the stolen car, he/she is going to tell you to get down on the ground (flat on your stomach), and might I suggest that you be in a real big hurry to comply and just lay down like they tell you to! You are then going to be told to spread your arms completely out to your sides, with your palms facing the sky and to face away from the officers. In most cases, all occupants of the vehicle will be extracted this way—until all occupants of the vehicle

CHAPTER 7: KNOCK IT OFF!

are taken into custody. This is department protocol... this is _not_ a case of you being harassed by the police! This is the standard operating procedures (SOP) of most law enforcement departments/agencies.

- Once the officer feels that he/she has extracted everyone from the vehicle, they will continue to shout commands at the vehicle, assuming that there is a final occupant in the vehicle that is not coming out. Again, this is standard operating procedures and is part of the department protocol for a felony traffic stop...and also for officer safety. These additional commands for other occupants to come out will normally be shouted out two to three times. You might also hear a command such as, "Police K-9...last occupant in the vehicle—exit the vehicle NOW with your hands in the air and face away from me or I'll release my dog!" Let me just share this little fun-fact with you while I have your attention...when you hear a police officer shout the word, "Dog," it's a **really** good time to just come out and surrender before that dog gets to that car, because they chew on things very well...if you know what I mean! I hope and I pray that you never have to experience this at all but, if you do, remembering these words that I shared with you can save your life! Once upon a time in my life, many years ago, I encountered a young man who was in the wrong place at the wrong time...doing *all* the wrong things. I was faced with detaining a motorist at gunpoint, who had just struck me with his vehicle and tried to evade arrest. As I was shouting commands at him to exit the vehicle with his hands straight up in the air, as I had been trained to do, this person did not want to surrender peacefully nor comply with my orders. With the intent of taking him into custody for Assault with a Deadly

Weapon (ADW, 245 PC), I continued to shout multiple commands at this person to comply and exit his vehicle to be placed under arrest. Rather than comply with my commands, this person turned his steering wheel in my direction and accelerated his vehicle at me, striking me a second time, as he continued his efforts to evade arrest. It was at that time that I had no other alternative but to discharge my weapon in an effort to overcome the threat against me and go home safely to my family... as I had been trained to do. For me, I wish I could turn back the hands of time and plead with the suspect a little while longer but, unfortunately, his hasty decision to accelerate his 4,000 pound vehicle towards me was a very terrible decision that ultimately caused him to pay the ultimate price for his actions. It also didn't help the situation by him being high on illegal drugs at the time. I sincerely believe that the level of illegal drugs in his system altered his ability to make rational and sound decisions...which ultimately played a role in his unfortunate demise. There was no joy that came out of living through that situation. In fact, if I could rewind the hands of time and re-live that day, I would've made up an excuse to call out sick and stay home that day! Even though my training and attention to duty allowed me to survive the attack, I feel like there were no real winners. It was a tremendous loss for his family and it was also a devastating hurt for me and my family as well, based on how we had to get through it. This is why I am begging anyone who reads this book to do what these police officers tell you to do when they have their guns drawn on you! Had this young man complied with my orders, he would surely still be here today but, for reasons I will never fully understand, he chose violence as the solution to escape his problems when all he had to do was listen. When police officers have their guns drawn on you, it's not the time to reach for your waistband because your pants are falling down. If you do that at the wrong moment...it just might be the very last thing you do in life! Is it embarrassing to be getting pulled out of a car at gunpoint by the police? Yes! Is it humiliating to be made to lie down on a filthy ground face down with your arms out to your side? Yes! Do you feel slightly violated when you are pounced on by several cops all trying to put handcuffs on you for something you feel like you did not do? Absolutely yes! But if you go along with the program, at least you live to see another day. There are many cases where the subject seemingly did go along with the program and still got killed by a police officer who may have used excessive force, but that's what courts are for. Argue it in court with a paid attorney, not on the street with 19 guns pointed at you! I'm begging you...DON'T RISK IT! Just do what they tell you to do and sort the rest out in a court of law.

At some point, we have to stop blaming other people for why our life is in the condition it's in and hold ourselves more accountable for what we KNOW we can be doing better! THAT'S how you become a leader—in your school, in your community, in your church and in the workplace. Change your mindset and your lifestyle will follow! Make better choices and you'll experience better outcomes!

You must always keep in mind that we live in an extremely judgmental society and, when you walk around sagging your pants, you are KILLING your own opportunities because the people in this world that have the ability and the influence to elevate you are immediately turned off by the fact that you don't even respect yourself. If you continue to demonstrate that you do not respect yourself, then why should other people respect you? Why should society respect you more than you respect yourself? Life doesn't work that way, in fact, it works just the opposite.

Sagging your pants like you don't care who sees you and what they think about you is a recipe for the most unsavory opportunities to come into your life, and you *do not* want that. When people lay their eyes on you each day, you want them to see that you are clean-shaven and well groomed. You want people to look at you and see that you care about your appearance and how you wear your clothing. You want people to see you and be able to tell that you have dignity and respect for yourself by how you conduct yourself out in public.

And to all of you men out there who are raising your young sons to become young men one day, stop planting seeds of worthlessness and failure into their young minds by making them feel guilty or ashamed for *crying*! KNOCK IT OFF!

So many men in our world today have compromised the mental and emotional health of their sons by saying things to them like, "Stop crying all the time! Crying is for babies and sissys!!" When you allow your child to grow up thinking that it is not okay to cry, you have no idea how much emotional damage you are doing to the future life that they have still not even learned how to define yet. If you sincerely love your son,

CHAPTER 7: KNOCK IT OFF!

SPEAK LIFE into his life so that he can allow himself to be taught how to succeed...rather than be taught how to fail.

Imagine if, later in his adult life, your son was physically abusive towards his girlfriend or his wife—all because he was never taught a more productive way to channel his anger or his emotional frustrations. When pressure builds up and has nowhere else to escape to, it explodes because the pressure is too great to be contained. How would you feel as a father if you learned that your son caused bodily harm to a woman because <u>*you*</u> taught him not to cry? You may not see the value in what I'm teaching you in this chapter but, one of these days, you will thank me for sharing what someone obviously never shared with you before you became a father.

Don't make your son suffer as a result of the father YOU never had! Empower your son to believe that he can achieve anything! Empower your son to believe in himself, especially when others will be lying in wait to watch him fail. Empower your son to stand ready to face the challenges of life with no fear, and with his head held up high! Empower your son to believe that, even when he will fall short from time to time, he is still a strong warrior who will one day obtain the victory he is fighting for—if he stays the course and does not give up on himself.

The moral to the story is simple...empower your son to constantly strive for greatness in all that he does. Don't take away your child's opportunity for a happy childhood or upbringing just because you feel like *you* didn't have one! Think about it!

DISCLAIMER: IF YOU ARE A TEENAGE GIRL, A YOUNG ADULT FEMALE OR A GROWN WOMAN, THIS SECTION BELOW IS SPECIFICALLY FOR YOU.

As a person who has always desired to be the father of a beautiful daughter someday, this section of the book is especially near and dear to my heart. In an effort to help teenage girls and young ladies better understand the dynamics of what I am going to say in this section, I am first going to dive right in and address the adult women who may be the mother of one or more daughters.

Women: Before you read any further, I want you to honestly clear your mind of anything that would be a hindrance or distraction to you right now. I'd like you to get somewhere peaceful and quiet where only you and God are allowed to be for just a few minutes. I am not about to ask you these questions with the intent of tearing you down or making you feel unnecessarily guilty…I am about to ask you these questions in an effort to light a fire underneath you that will move you into action, with regard to addressing complex and hurtful issues that you may have been running away from for far too long! If you feel like these questions do not apply to you, praise the Lord, you are the exception to the rule. However, if the shoe fits, I want you to wear it…and keep it on until the day that your journey to complete healing is achieved!

I want you to go into deep, deep thought and go back to that time in your life when you were just a little girl who only cared about cartoons and birthday cake. Go back as far as you can remember and think about all of the happy times of your childhood. I want you to think about all of the fun places you went to and all of your friends or other family members who may have shared those experiences with you. Can you see the little girl yet? Does she still look the way you remember her, or does she now look different in your mind?

If you can now visualize that little girl from your childhood, does she still look happy like you remember her, or does she look sad? Now I'd like you to tell *yourself* the truth. Did somebody that you knew back then hurt that little girl inside of you? Did somebody that you once knew back then deceive or trick that little girl inside of you? Did somebody that you knew back then make that happy little girl inside of you feel scared or terrified? Did someone that you once knew back then take advantage of that little girl's trust? Who was it? More importantly, what did you ever do about it?

Is there someone from back then that you trusted to protect you from harm, yet they failed you miserably? Who was it that let you down? Who failed to protect you from the person or the people that hurt you? If any of these questions have moved you to a place of anger, hurt, disgust or even tearful discomfort, then it is a sign that there is some level of emotional or psychological trauma still lingering in your adult life, from your past, that you have never dealt with. From the day that these hurtful things compromised the innocence of your childhood, to now, these issues have been ignored, yet stored in the *"Drafts"* folder of your subconscious mind.

I want to admonish you that, even though you may have not yet dealt with the hurts and pains of your past, it is not too late to take that leap of faith to reach out to someone that you trust for help and guidance to TRULY begin your healing process. I sincerely hope that there can be something said in this book that will uplift you to the point of desiring to chase your rightful opportunity to heal from the scars of your past, while you are still on the time side of life. It is my hope that you will not continue to let your *past* have power and dominion over the richly rewarding *future* that is waiting for you to claim. If you don't heal from your past, sooner than later, you are going to sit back and watch your own daughter experience the same exact pain and trauma that you were made to experience… because you won't know how to best protect her from it—the same way someone failed to protect YOU.

The preceding questions and concerns are sparked by the current social behaviors that are seen daily across all forms of social media. It pains my heart to no end when I get on social media and see young girls and grown women devaluing themselves by posting overly provocative and downright half-naked pictures of themselves online for the world to see. Have you seen this? The next time you see someone post a provocative picture of themselves on social media, pay very close attention to the photos they post or look through their photo albums. I guarantee you that you will find even more photos just like the ones you see being posted.

From a male perspective, when I look on social media and see photos of grown women in public restrooms, as well as restrooms within their home, taking selfies while sporting suggestive attire, it really makes me wonder why they find it so

CHAPTER 7: KNOCK IT OFF!

urgent and so important to seize the perfect restroom moment to show the world that they are in the restroom taking pictures. To me, that is the behavior of a person who is crying out for attention and, please, don't get me wrong… men do it too!

This type of behavior really does beg these questions: "What voids in your life are you trying to fill by exploiting yourself on social media? What is the deeply-rooted issue in your life that is causing you to have such a desire to have people on social media validate you and determine *your* worth? Do you honestly feel that posting a multitude of photos on social media with your breasts exposed in almost every picture defines who you truly are, and what you have to offer to society?

If you are a woman in a leadership position in your organization, how do you feel something like this affects how your peers and subordinates will view you as a leader in a professional setting? Did something bad happen in your past that still has you feeling unimportant to yourself today? Forget about what the world thinks about you…what do YOU think about you? There's something missing in your life, if exploiting yourself on social media doesn't even bother you.

Young girls: *Do not* follow in the footsteps of the women before you who failed to teach you how to identify your value and your self-worth. You will eventually regret it if you choose not to listen to these words of wisdom! If a young boy or a young man doesn't love and appreciate you for who you already are, then don't you dare lower your standards just so that you can end up with a boy that is ultimately going to prove to you that he was never worth your time in the first place!

Identify your value; understand your worth. Don't ever compromise who you truly are for who other people want you to be. Don't ever do that! If you lose an opportunity to be with a boy or a young man that doesn't add value to your life…you have actually gained, you haven't lost anything. Carry yourself as a Queen; carry yourself with a degree of dignity that speaks loudly enough for you that you do not even have to waste your breath telling others what you are all about.

No matter who failed to take you under their wing to teach you and show you what being a respectable young lady is all about, that doesn't mean that you have to degrade yourself by advertising your body to the world, and offering yourself as a living sacrifice to boys or young men that are not even deserving of being in your company! You are more valuable than you have been giving yourself credit for, but it's not too late for you to change your mindset and change your way of thinking about the best ways that you can understand and identify your value!

Find an older woman in your circle of friends, family members or associates who can mentor you and take you under their wing to help groom you into the flawless work of art that God designed you to be. Stop surrounding yourself with other girls or women that have no ambition in life to be anything greater than what they already are. Whatever type of woman you hope to be in the future, you need to start surrounding yourself with that caliber of woman IMMEDIATELY, so that their wisdom and their knowledge about how to live a rewarding life can start rubbing off on you. Always surround yourself with people who are doing greater things than you so that they can be a source of strength and encouragement to you and empower you to strive to be where you desire to be in your own personal life.

Again, I don't say these things to be demeaning or confrontational, I am simply exposing the reality of how social media, and many other advancements in modern day technology has caused many of us to forget who we are and what we stand for! Within my own personal circle of friends, family and associates, social media has been regarded as *"the devil's playground!"* You do not need me to identify the horrific, distasteful and unethical mess that is posted on social media every day. You see exactly what I see.

If there are still unresolved, hurtful and painful issues from your past that still haunt you, for whatever reason, you must seek to get professional help for those toxic emotions so that you can move forward with your life in a healthier, more positive manner. If you continue staring your past in the face every day, you will never see your future!

What if the unresolved scars of your past are the very things that are preventing you from being a better leader today? Just what if? Is it worth humbling yourself and swallowing your pride to allow yourself a chance at a better quality of life? I believe it absolutely is. If you are finding out the hard way that you are struggling with successfully getting your children through the oftentimes dark challenges of life that have landed at their feet, it's primarily because YOU have not taken the time out to successfully overcome and be delivered from the dark challenges of life that are still holding YOU back from being a better version of yourself!

You can never fix another person until you have mastered the importance of fixing you FIRST. No matter what a great parent you are, or what a great leader you proclaim to be, you cannot change people...people can only change themselves when they're finally able to admit that there's a need to do so.

As responsible mothers and fathers who have children that are watching and listening to everything that we say and do, we must step up to the plate and hold ourselves accountable for areas in our lives where we can make a more positive impact on the lives of our children and on our children's children. Regardless of what you think you know about leadership; regardless of the leadership principles you may have been taught decades ago; regardless of how many leadership conventions and workshops you've attended in the past; regardless of the basic, fundamental elements of leadership that you think is still the *"cure-all"* method of leading, I submit to you that today...it's a new day! We must continue to remind ourselves that, in today's society that we are all still learning to adjust to...it's a new day!

If we do not start becoming better examples and better life-coaches to our children, all we are teaching them how to do is fail and be dependent on us for the rest of their lives.

CHAPTER 8

Building Your Financial Future

In this chapter, I am going to teach you what I wholeheartedly believe no one has ever taught you all throughout grade school, including your parents and grandparents. Regardless of what you think…regardless of what other people think…regardless of what you've heard and regardless of if you believe it or not—*residual income* is the most powerful form of income on planet Earth. Period! The only other thing more powerful than residual income is *passive residual income*.

If you are serious about having a healthy financial future, you had better get serious RIGHT NOW about learning how to acquire residual income! Knowing what I know now, I am so upset that none of my so-called "teachers" in grade school ever taught me about residual income at any time during all of my years of school. If teachers in our society are paid to teach our children things that will allow them to get ahead in life, why are they not teaching our children about the power of residual income or passive residual income? It almost feels like a set-up for failure, rather than higher learning.

If you forget anything else that I have written in this book, trust me when I tell you, you cannot afford to forget ANYTHING that I am about to teach you in this chapter. Mastering the concepts that I am teaching you in this chapter can be the difference between you working for money the rest of your life *vs.* making your money work for you.

There are two standard ways of earning money—**linear income** and **residual income**. *Linear income* is when you are trading time for dollars. This means, when you go to your job and you work 40 hours per week, you will eventually get a paycheck every week or every two weeks. This is an example of trading time for dollars; when you do the work, your employer pays you. When you stop doing the work, your employer stops paying you!

Residual income works just the opposite. With residual income, you only do the work ONE TIME, yet you get paid on that work over and over and over and over and over and over again… without having to repeat the efforts of the original work that you did! Did you get that? Let me say it again, but pay close attention this time because NOW you will have to start stepping out of your comfort zone in order to allow this information to reshape the way you think about your income and your expenses. With residual income, you only do the work **ONE TIME**, yet you get paid on that work *over and over and over and over and over and over again*…without having to repeat the efforts of the original work that you did a long time ago!

Let me give you a more applicable example of how residual income works and, while I'm explaining this to you, also

CHAPTER 8: BUILDING YOUR FINANCIAL FUTURE

understand that there are multiple layers and levels to residual income, so pay very close attention. This may be a chapter that you might find yourself reading over and over and over again, until you grasp the concept of how residual income truly works—and how it can literally change your life FOREVER!

For the sake of these examples, I want you to think of a *"residual"* as a *"royalty."* Royalties are an essential element of residual income, and here is how they work for you in order to create money. Notice I said, "Here is how **they work for you**!" With regards to residuals (or royalties) that are derived from the music business, we will use Michael Jackson as the example in this scenario.

Back in the early 1980's, Michael Jackson wrote and performed a song called "Beat It." To give you a chance to see dollars and cents in this example, let's just say that the single "Beat It" sold 2 million copies around the world. If each single sold at $14.99 per copy sold, that would be a net value of $29, 980,000.00. Keep in mind that is only revenue that Michael Jackson would have earned just from the sales of the single release alone.

Also keep in mind that, once the album or single started to sell that many copies, Michael Jackson went on tour and performed those songs and attracted millions of people to come to his concerts. Now let's look at another example of the *"additional"* money that Michael Jackson made off of that same song, "Beat It." Since Michael Jackson wrote the song "Beat It," and performed it, he would be legally entitled to collect the following payments:

- Publishing Royalties (additional money)
- Artist Royalties (additional money)
- Performance Royalties (additional money)
- Mechanical Royalties (additional money)

Please keep in mind that the four types of royalties shown above are sources of income IN ADDITION TO the $29, 980, 000.00 that I already mentioned to you from the sales of his single "Beat It." The royalty percentages in each category will always vary based on how contractual agreements and stipulations are worded but, for the most part, this is an exceptionally large amount of money that Michael Jackson earned off of JUST ONE SONG!! Are you getting this? Are you honestly getting this? ONE SONG! Based on what I just showed you in this scenario, don't you wish that YOU were the one who wrote the song "Beat It?"

Not only did Michael Jackson earn residual income off of all forms of the royalties mentioned above, he would have also had the ability to earn money from concession stand sales, merchandising items at his concerts (i.e., souvenir T-shirts, posters, hats, books, etc.). Because of its multi-faceted complexity in making people understand how royalties and residual income works within the music industry, this is something that I usually explain in greater detail when I am speaking to a large group of people at a paid venue.

Another way you can quickly earn residual income, if you are coachable to the organization's marketing plan, is by

CHAPTER 8: BUILDING YOUR FINANCIAL FUTURE

getting yourself involved with **network marketing**! Network marketing is also oftentimes referred to as *multi-level marketing* (MLM). If you decide to take a closer look at a network marketing company, I highly recommend that you do as much research on the products and services that the company offers before you invest any of your time or money to get started with whatever company you decide to be a part of.

In my strongest opinion, stay away from companies that will require you to carry around large quantities of unnecessary merchandise that you will have no room to store, and that most people will probably not be interested in buying from you. Find a company that has a product or service that most people either need, want, or cannot live without. You always want to partner with a network marketing company that has products or services that can literally sell themselves! By doing this, you'll be working *smart* and not hard. You also want to be sure that the start-up costs are very minimal, but make sure that their marketing plan allows you to recoup your investment costs as fast as humanly possible. In other words, find the network marketing company that has the most affordable cost to get started and allows you to make the most money in return. There's nothing wrong with working hard but, in network marketing, the mindset is always to work SMART...NOT HARD!

If there are still any that exist in *today's* society, try to partner with a network marketing company that offers their customers discounted rates on things such as: natural gas, electricity, insurance, telecommunications or other technology based services, legal services, real estate or financial planning services.

With the economy being as unstable as it is right now, financial planning services would be an excellent place to start for those trying to supplement their income to make some extra money outside of their primary career. I also highly recommend that you look for the companies that sell products to consumers that have impressive health benefits. Health and nutrition are booming industries right now, so that's also an excellent place to start.

Before you decide to get involved, do your due diligence in making sure that the network marketing organization is a "ground-floor" opportunity for you. Also make sure that the company has not gone public yet. If you are confident that you are getting in on a ground-floor opportunity, and the company is still privately held, you stand to make a staggering amount of income (as a return on your investment) if you position yourself in time and you build a strong organization of other people who are also making money with you before the company announces that they are going public. Network marketing is all about being in business *for* yourself, but not *by* yourself. Remember that concept in every phase of building your own personal downline within that organization.

Another reason why I think it is extremely important to consider partnering with a reputable network marketing company is because, at some point in their marketing plan is the ability for your money to grow *exponentially*. Exponential growth simply means, the further away something gets from its origin the bigger it spreads. If you do not know what **exponential growth** is, and how it can easily translate into thousands and

CHAPTER 8: BUILDING YOUR FINANCIAL FUTURE

thousands and hundreds of thousands of dollars, you need to have an expert within that network marketing organization sit you down and explain it to you step by step.

Once you learn and master the concept of creating multiple streams of residual income, and also watching those growth-spurts grow exponentially, your financial worries can easily become a worry of the past! I highly recommend that you go to the Google search engine and type in: *exponential growth charts*. Keep in mind that I mentioned earlier, if you are going to decide to utilize a network marketing organization to create streams of residual or passive residual income, make sure that it is a ground-floor opportunity! If you confirm that it is a ground-floor opportunity, then use that ground-floor theory as your point of origin to begin making money.

Once you have this concept in place, all of the exponential growth on the charts you research should be pointing in an upward direction. If you decide to create an exponential growth chart that shows yourself at the very top, then, as your organization continues to grow, your exponential growth should point downward and get bigger and bigger as it continues to grow downward.

Once you partner into a network marketing company that you feel comfortable with, YOU become the origin of whatever NEW money that will find its way into your bank account. If you follow the marketing plan the way that it is explained to you, once you start growing your own business within the organization, your money will begin to grow exponentially. Again, that just means that the further away something gets from its origin, the bigger it grows. If you work hard for six months to a year, and you build your team correctly, your money will begin to start growing exponentially and you won't be able to stop it...even if you try to! If you sincerely desire to acquire financial freedom, you need to start becoming more financially literate as well, and understand how money works.

WARNING: Once your friends and family members find out that you have already done so, or are interested in partnering with a network marketing company, they are likely going to try to discourage you. No matter what happens, stick to your plan to make the best of EVERY opportunity available to you along your journey of building multiple streams of residual income and pursuing YOUR financial freedom. Identify your "WHY" and always remind yourself of why you are pursuing financial freedom. Is it because you want to retire your parents early because you are tired of seeing them work at their old age? Is it because you are tired of having no money left over at the end of your month? Is it because you're a single parent who just wants to generate some extra money to be able to take your kids on fun trips? Is it because you're tired of working your fingers to the bone for a company that does not appreciate your hard work? Or, is it simply because you are sick and tired of being sick and tired?

Whatever reasons fit your "WHY," those will be the reasons that you *must* keep in the forefront of your mind at all times as you are working towards your financial goals...and just your goals in general.

CHAPTER 8: BUILDING YOUR FINANCIAL FUTURE

Don't buy other people's opinions about what you should be doing with your life and *why* you should be doing it. I have always been of the belief that, if you keep buying other people's opinions, you will ultimately be buying *their* lifestyle! If they are not driving the car of their dreams, don't worry yourself about their opinions. If they are not living in their dream home, don't worry yourself about *their* opinions. If they are not debt free for themselves, then stop allowing yourself to fall victim to how *they* think you should be pursuing your financial freedom. If they are not already living the kind of life that you aspire to live someday, then don't give life to *their* way of thinking.

If you ever make a decision to relocate to another country to live, it is very important that you take the necessary time to learn the language spoken in that country. If you are going to decide to move to France one day, you need to be ready to start learning how to speak French so that you will be prepared to communicate with the locals, and also be able to understand their native tongues. Equally, if you are going to decide to improve your financial future, you MUST be able to speak and understand financial languages! There is no getting around this, as you prepare to recondition the way you have always thought about money.

In today's society, primarily due to the ongoing evolution of the internet and cyber technology, the English language has literally been transformed into a totally different way in which people communicate with each other. Today we communicate with each other using acronyms like: LOL, OMG, IKR, WYD, ROTFL, BFF, TMI, WTH or even BTW. If you are truly trying to level up and take better control of your financial future, you need to start learning acronyms like: APR, ROI, 401K, FICO, IRA and IPO. If you are fluent in understanding the first set of acronyms, but not the second set of acronyms, your priorities are completely out of order!

You also need to start educating yourself on the differences between **assets** *vs.* **liabilities; principal** *vs.* **interest** and **hard inquiries** *vs.* **soft inquiries**. I could easily explain it to you in this chapter but, if I were to make it that easy for you, I would be preventing you from taking on that leadership role to go out and research it for yourself. I've given you more than enough information to begin your research…now it's up to you to be a leader and research it for yourself and make the information work for you!

The next thing that I want to draw your undivided attention to is something that most of us did not learn until it was already too late. If you have not already mastered this important lesson in life, you must get very good at understanding how to build and protect your *credit* and your *credit score!* Your credit score is the rise and fall of every exciting and worthwhile event you will ever want to experience in your lifetime.

When you go to a car dealership thinking that you're going to drive off in that new car that you want…when you are ready to start the process of buying that house you want to move into…and even when you are ready to move out of your parents' house and into your own apartment, everything that you will or will not be able to obtain is going to depend on how strong your credit score is.

CHAPTER 8: BUILDING YOUR FINANCIAL FUTURE

If you do not understand what a credit score is, and also what credit scores are good *vs.* which ones are bad, I highly recommend that you go to the Google search engine and type in: *credit score ranges*. Once you do that, you can research for yourself which credit scores are looked upon favorably by lenders *vs.* which credit scores will get you nowhere with lenders.

If you have already established credit with one or more lenders, here are some excellent credit tips that will always help you to keep your credit in good standing and protect your credit worthiness. If you get a statement (credit card bill) in the mail that is asking you to pay a minimum payment amount of $25.00, always make an effort to pay an extra $10.00 or $15.00 in addition to that minimum payment. Whenever you pay more than the minimum amount that your creditor is asking you to pay, you are showing them that you are responsible with repaying what you owe them for lending you the money in the first place. In this example, $25.00 is only the "minimum" payment amount due. Just because $25.00 is your "minimum" payment due, it does not mean that you cannot pay *more* than the $25.00, it simply means that you cannot pay any "less" than that amount.

In addition to paying a little bit more than the minimum amount that is being asked of you, also make sure you are paying your credit card bills on time! Not paying your credit card bills on time will cause your credit score to go down slightly. If you make a habit of not paying your credit card bills on time, this can make your credit score go down much more, because now you are showing your lenders a pattern of financial irresponsibility. Every time that your lender receives your payment late, your lender can legally charge you a late payment fee…which is an additional cost added on to what you still previously owed.

If your payment due date is on the 15th of every month, get into the habit of paying your bill a few days early—or even a week or two early. This shows your lender that, not only did you pay more than the minimum amount they were asking, you also paid the amount you owed before it was even due which, again, shows your lender that you are responsible with repaying what you owe them. This is yet another way to keep your credit score at a healthy rating and, in some cases, can even cause your lender to offer you a higher line of credit.

Another way credit card companies make money off of people is by charging an *over the limit fee*. If your credit card company approves your application for credit, most lenders will start you off with an opening line of credit consisting of anywhere between $300.00 to up to $500.00 worth of available credit. If your available credit limit is only $300.00, show your lender that you can be responsible with that $300.00 credit limit for a whole year. If you can make it past the six or seven month mark with making your repayments on time, a lot of lenders will offer you a higher line of credit as a way to reward you for making your payments on time. However, the first time you use your credit card to make a purchase, try to stay away from purchasing things that are too close to your maximum limit!

If you purchase a set of power tools that are on sale for $299.00, then that is *__not__* a smart purchase to make if your credit limit is only $300.00. You have to remember that $299.00 is the sale price *"before"* tax is applied to that sale. Once the tax has been applied to

CHAPTER 8: BUILDING YOUR FINANCIAL FUTURE

your purchase, your grand total for that set of power tools will be approximately $323.67, which will take you over your maximum credit limit by $23.67. Once this happens, not only do you have to pay back the $323.67, you will also have to pay an over the limit fee for making a purchase for more than what your available credit limit was.

This additional, over the limit fee is normally between $25.00 to $39.00. Try to only use your credit cards in cases of emergency or when you are 100% certain that you will be able to make slightly more than the minimum payment once your credit card statement arrives in the mail. These are just some simple, common tips you can practice every month to try to improve your credit score. You should also sign up for credit monitoring that will allow you to login and check your credit score from time to time.

The last thing I'd like to educate you about in this chapter is the importance of learning how to use various tax shelters to your benefit. A **tax shelter** is a method in which the state and local government will give you a calculated discount on any taxes that you would ordinarily owe after you file your tax return each year. Since I have already used it in previous examples, I am going to use network marketing as a focal point to help you better understand how a tax shelter works.

The moment you sign up to partner with a network marketing company or organization, you have immediately started a home-based *"business."* Once you establish that you have a home-based "business," you can now start saving your receipts to use as your proof that you have business expenses that you can now write-off on your income taxes.

If your home-based business involves marketing products to consumers that have impressive health benefits, for every product that you buy at your wholesale distributor cost, you can give those receipts to your tax accountant and they will use it on your income tax return as proof that you have an out-of-pocket expense for your home-based business. Depending on other factors that are outlined in your tax filing, you can get a little bit of a bigger refund on your income taxes, as opposed to if you did not have any business expenses to claim. In other cases, you still might owe, but you might not owe as much as you would have if you were not under this type of tax shelter. Don't just write-off things just for the sake of writing them off. Always have integrity about the out-of-pocket expenses you are going to claim on your taxes because, if you get audited and it is determined that some of your write-off expenses are not eligible for a deduction, you could find yourself in big trouble with the tax board or with the IRS.

I hope this chapter provided you with enough information to see how you can get your finances back on track and how you can build or strengthen your credit score in the process. Your credit is the foundation of everything you will want to obtain in your life, so take good care of your credit by always striving to keep your credit score in the 690 to 800 range. Get into the habit of going to the home page of your credit card carrier's website to find out additional tips that you can practice to keep your credit in good standing. You can thank me later!

CHAPTER 9

Never Give Up

To everyone who has taken the time to read this book, I first want to thank you for your valuable time in considering the information that was put on my heart to share with you! I sincerely hope that this book has made you feel WORTHY rather than worthless. I hope this book has UPLIFTED you rather than knocked you down. I hope, trust and pray that, that this book has EMPOWERED you rather than devalued you or tore you down.

I truly realize that there was quite a bit of positive, enlightening information that I have shared with you up until this point. However, I also realize that there were some unfavorable and uncomfortable topics that were discussed. I have always been of the belief that, once we identify our failures, we must always hold ourselves accountable for making an overt effort to *right* our *wrongs* and push forward towards success.

Sometimes, as leaders, we have to swallow our pride and deal with the "elephant in the room," whether we want to or not. This is the point in our leadership where we lift up that rug that we've been sweeping all of our problems up under—and we sift through the debris to start cleaning up the messes that WE helped to create by our failure to lead and also our ongoing willingness to continue ignoring the broken areas in our organization that has needed fixing for a very long time.

For those of us who are passionate about either being leaders, or learning *how* to become leaders, we have to be willing to strip ourselves *of* ourselves and become humble servants to those around us who may not know how to lead. As leaders, we must be willing to be their voice and speak out against unfairness in the workplace. Enough is enough! As leaders, we must also be willing to be the voice of those in our society who feel constantly defeated, forgotten, beat down, black-listed, silenced and hopeless.

As leaders, we have to always be in the spirit of giving, training, improving, empowering, inspiring, uplifting and encouraging. The very moment that we stop showing empathy and compassion towards the very people who help us shine, by all of their hard work, we stop being leaders at that very moment. There is a very distinct difference between leadership and a dictatorship. I know there are times when you feel defeated, but don't give up! I know there are times when, as a leader in your organization, you feel like you don't have the needed support of your upper management team, but don't give up. I know that, as a leader, there are times when you want to just quit because you are constantly feeling like you're the only leader in the office who has integrity, but don't give up! You're doing great…keep going! Don't give up!

CHAPTER 9: NEVER GIVE UP

You were raised by wolves and bears because your mother abandoned you when you were a child, and that damaged you emotionally! Ok, I get it...but how much longer will you *choose* to remain damaged? Your father was never there for you during some of the most critical and impressionable periods in your life! Trust me, if anyone understands the abandonment of a father, I do. I know that made you feel worthless and empty inside, but how many more years are you going to *choose* to keep on singing that same old song out loud for the world to hear—repeatedly? When is it finally going to be time to let go of those hurtful emotions and leave them in the past where they belong? If you're struggling to find the answer to that question, let me give you a little bit of encouragement.

TODAY is the day that you need to finally wave *goodbye* to the pains, hurts, disappointments and tribulations of your past and start positioning yourself to acquire a more solid foundation for securing and stabilizing your future! If you continue to *choose* to focus on your past, then you will never be in a position to see your future! Every track star who has won an Olympic Gold Medal, won the race by looking FORWARD... not by looking backwards. How do you ever expect to win your races in life if you continue to focus on what is already behind you? The answer is quite simple...you can't! Stop doubting yourself and putting yourself down for what your past never gave you! Stop putting yourself down just because you haven't acquired the things in life that you feel like you should have obtained by now. Everyone's journey in this life cannot be the same! Everyone's goal and purpose in life is not always going to be in alignment with one another. The things in life that work for other people are not always meant to work for YOU!

Your future is counting on you to re-engage with life's endless possibilities for you, so that you can start marking some of your most important goals off of your bucket list and continue making forward progress! You can do it…you got this! How do you expect others to believe in you when you can't even demonstrate that YOU believe in you? If you refuse to take that first, pivotal leap of faith towards reaching your dreams and achieving your goals, then how will you ever know what could have been? You won't! You will never know how successful you will have been at something until you overcome your fears of making the effort to obtain it. FEAR is—False Evidence Appearing Real. Do not continue buying into the false evidence that suggests you have nothing positive to look forward to in this life. Do not continue to buy into the false reality that causes you to doubt your gifts, talents and creative abilities. It's a new day today!

Start thinking outside of that imaginary box you've been trapped in for all of your life, and start dreaming again. Most people in this world today are going nowhere fast because, for whatever their circumstances or reasons are, they just literally stopped dreaming! I can't say this enough…if you are still reading this book, IT'S A NEW DAY TODAY! If you started reading this book yesterday and are still reading it again today…it's a new day!

Today you have a fresh start to having a better day than yesterday. Today you have a new opportunity to be a better mother, a better father, a better son, a better daughter, a better grandparent, a better pastor, a better husband and a better wife. Whatever is broken in your life today, fix it today because tomorrow is not promised. In all endeavors of your life, seek to be at peace with as many people as you possibly can. When you are at peace within yourself, it becomes just a little bit easier to be at peace with other people around you that you have to share this world with.

You are not going to always get along with every single person you come in contact with, but don't let other people's negative outlook on life dictate the type of positive person you know YOU ought to be. As you strive for goals in your life, there will be times when you will fall flat on your face and feel like a failure…but please don't give up! There will be times when you will go to friends and family members with a high level of happiness and excitement about a new business venture that you are going to start, but not all of them are going to share your excitement or support you…but please don't give up! There will be times in your life when your failures will seem to be greater than your accomplishments, but please don't give up on yourself!

Sometimes the greatest blessings in your life will not appear until you have boldly endured the worst possible circumstances in your life. When you feel like there's no hope left in what you're striving for and why you are striving for it, just hold on to your faith and know that you are worthy of greatness; expect victory at every turn in your life and, in due time, victory will be placed at your feet. As your level of confidence and your belief in yourself continues to grow stronger, the confidence and belief in you from others will grow stronger as well. If you don't learn anything else in this chapter, know and understand that no matter how badly people around you want to see you become successful, no one else can want it more for you than you want it for yourself.

Acknowledgments

Where do I even begin? With all of the extremely challenging things that I have gone through over the past 14 years, this section of the book is seemingly the most difficult to write. If you truly knew the magnitude of what I have overcome in the past decade or so, maybe, just maybe you would understand how it feels to have the weight of the world lifted up off of your shoulders. When I made a decision over twenty years ago to live my life in the public eye, I knew it was not going to be easy, but I also never thought that it was going to be THIS hard. For everyone that God put in my life, and allowed to cross my path, I want to thank you **_all_** from the very bottom of my heart, for standing by my side through some of the darkest, scariest and most difficult moments of my life!

There is just no possible way that I could have EVER made it this far along my journey without your love, without your support, without your encouragement, without your words of wisdom, without your faith in me, without your belief in my vision and without you being my strength during times when I was too weak to even believe in myself. This book has been a long time coming and, by the grace and favor of an almighty and trustworthy God, it has finally come to pass and has manifested into a reality. I want to thank everyone who played a vital role in feeding me the wisdom and the knowledge I needed along the way to be an even better father to my amazing children—understanding that they are watching everything that I do and listening to everything that I say. To my incredible children...I want to publicly offer my sincere thanks to you for being patient with me during our most difficult times—when all I was striving to do is protect you and give you the best life possible, no matter what challenges landed at our feet. Even when I felt like a failure as your father, you still showered me with the best hugs and the warmest smiles that said, "I trust you, Dad." If I could only make mention of one more monumental figure in my life, it would have to be my heroic mother!

Mom...even as a grown man, it scares me to no end to imagine where I'd be today if I didn't have you in my life. There's just no way humanly possible that I can begin to describe my appreciation for you, for all you have done for me in my life. As a single mother doing the job of two people, I admire your strength and your leadership in how you always encouraged me to be the best I can possibly be, and to always put God at the forefront of every plan or goal. There are so many people in this world who no longer have an opportunity to tell their mother how much they love them, because they have passed on. I am using this platform to publicly tell you how much I love you and thank God for you. Looking back, I know that I have not always made the best choices nor all the right decisions all the time, but I hope that this accomplishment fairly and accurately represents all of the hard work that you put into raising me to be the man I am today.

To all the haters that said this book was all talk and no action... this one's for you! With your negative energy and your negative outlook on my vision, it was just the right amount of inspiration I needed to push me over the finish-line. Thank you for leaving me hanging and demonstrating your lack of support for the positive ways in which I choose to inspire and empower my community with this book. Without your negative outlook and your pointless efforts towards trying to derail my progress, I would have never been able to show the world how to turn negative energy into positive outcomes...so thank you for being a part of the process. To everyone who chose to fall for all the negative things that the internet had to say about me, rather than be a leader and take time to get to know *the real me* for yourself, thank you for helping to push me to greatness! Without you hating on me so hard, for reasons that even YOU don't fully understand, I would have never been able to finish this book. For the haters that I haven't even met yet, believe me when I tell you that I really need your continued support to get to the next goal, so please...keep on hating on the things that I do so that I can keep on using your negative energy as fuel to get to my next blessing and destination in life. If you are still reading this book at this point, and you also have haters that are criticizing everything that you do, and always talking about you behind your back, do not let your haters steal your joy just because they don't have any to enjoy for themselves!

When you realize that you have haters that are hating on you for no good reason, you have a duty and an obligation to strive to reach your goals *that* much faster, so that you can give your haters something new and exciting to talk about. Understand that, what a hater fails to realize is, they give you power over their life by hating on you, and they're not even smart enough to understand what they're doing to cut off their own blessings. If they hate you so much, why do they always have your name in their mouth speaking on you? I'm persuaded to believe that they're hating on you because they see something special in *you* that they don't see in themselves. I'm persuaded to believe that they're hating on you because they envy the fact that you have supportive friends and family members and they do not. I'm persuaded to believe that they're hating on you because they see that you have gifts and talents that they don't have. So, when you discover that someone is hating on you as you continue to strive to reach your goals, understand that they're just doing their job. With that in mind, you do YOUR job and prove them wrong about every hateful and ignorant thing that they have ever said about you.

Sometimes you won't know who your haters are until the very last minute. As you are down in the trenches pursuing your dreams, your haters will be nowhere to be found when you need support along the way but, when you finally blow up…they'll be all in your face saying to you, "I knew you could do it!" If you find that you are able to take away something positive from this book, share it with as many people as you care about so that they can be blessed too. Thank you for your valuable time in reading this book and allowing me to share my stories with you!

IN LOVING MEMORY

Police Chief John M. Lawrence, Sr.
May 17, 1933–May11, 2016

As talented as God has made me with the gift of written expression, there are just no words in the human language to describe how very much I miss you. I miss hearing your voice, I miss hearing your impromptu sense of humor, I miss coming over to the house to watch old western movies with you, I miss coming over to the house to lay around lazily across the couch—just to sit and unwind from life with you...just to be in your presence. It was always difficult for me to refer to you as merely my Godfather, because you meant so much more to me than that. I regret that I never seized the opportunity to tell you, in person, that you are the father I never had! Whenever I faced a hardship of any kind, you were there to stand in the gap to help me out. Whenever I was down in the dumps, and being hard on myself because I was not where I wanted to be in life, you were constantly by my side to remind me, "It's always darkest before the dawn!" From the day God allowed us to come into each other's life, you always had an uplifting and encouraging word to share with me. Those moments were times in my life where your encouragement served as a moment for me to mentally recharge my batteries, so that I was less likely to give up on my dreams…and I thank you for those selfless moments you took out of your days to believe in me, when there were times I was not strong enough to believe in myself. Because of all the things that you have taught me about life, I am now using this book as a platform to teach others how to become the best versions of themselves…and to teach them how to identify and understand their value and their self-worth. My love and admiration for you was NEVER about what the family name represented, as I would always remind you, "I loved you for the fact that you chose to love me first!" That alone has always been worth far more to me than the Hollywood lifestyle could ever have offered. Thank you, Dad, for giving me some of the best memories of my life. Thank you for stepping up to the plate and seeing the value in me to want to take me under your wing and adopt me as your godson. I miss you more than words will ever allow me to repeat, and I wish so much that you were here with me to FINALLY be able to witness my "dawn" of what you always said would come to pass in my life. I admire you for all of your achievements while you were here, and working your way up to Chief of Police, and I thank you for your service to our country as a military veteran. You were truly one of the best and, in my book, you still are. Rest well, Dad.

Eternally,
Dameon K. Wroe
Godson

NOTES:

NOTES:

www.ingramcontent.com/pod-product-compliance
Lightning Source LLC
Chambersburg PA
CBHW050552300426
44112CB00013B/1883